# The Book Club Companion

# The Book Club Companion

## Fostering Strategic Readers in the Secondary Classroom

Cindy O'Donnell-Allen

**HEINEMANN**
Portsmouth, NH

**Heinemann**
A division of Reed Elsevier Inc.
361 Hanover Street
Portsmouth, NH 03801–3912
www.heinemann.com

*Offices and agents throughout the world*

© 2006 by Cindy O'Donnell-Allen

**Library of Congress Cataloging-in-Publication Data**
O'Donnell-Allen, Cindy.
  The book club companion : fostering strategic readers in the secondary classroom / Cindy O'Donnell-Allen.
    p. cm.
  Includes bibliographical references.
    ISBN 0-325-00829-9 (alk. paper)
    ISBN-13: 978-0-325-00829-5
    1. Book clubs (Discussion groups).  2. Reading (Secondary).  3. Youth
  —Books and reading.    I. Title.

  LC6631.O36 2006
  428.4071'2—dc22                                           2006018769

*Editor:* Jim Strickland
*Production editor:* Sonja S. Chapman
*Cover design:* Cat & Mouse Design, Catherine Hawkes
*Compositor:* Argosy
*Manufacturing:* Steve Bernier

Printed in the United States of America on acid-free paper
10   09   08   07   06     RRD     1   2   3   4   5

For Lexie and Lynley,
Austen and Will,
whom I would deem amazing
even if they didn't belong to me

# Contents

# Foreword

Ten years ago I had the extraordinary experience of observing one of Cindy O'Donnell-Allen's classrooms for an entire year. At the time, she'd recently completed her master's degree at the University of Oklahoma where I taught, and she was contemplating a return to begin her doctorate. Cindy had been among the OU College of Education's most distinguished graduates: She received their competitive and prestigious Outstanding Senior award while working on her initial certification, and was among the core leaders of the Oklahoma Writing Project at a very early career stage. She founded the OWP's teacher-research group (which ultimately became the focus of her doctoral dissertation—see O'Donnell-Allen 2001) and was a high-demand presenter at both Advanced Placement conferences and OWP consultations. While I had studied students from her class before—she was "Ms. McDonald" in Smagorinsky (1997)—I had never undertaken a full-blown ethnography that would enable me to observe one class' complete set of meetings from August to May. Was I ever in for a treat.

When you watch someone teach for an entire year (her school worked on a block schedule, with classes meeting every other day for the full year), you see it all: days when there's magic in the air, days when it seems everyone's got the flu, days that go by too fast, days that seem as though they'll never end. Along with a second observer I was able to hire with a grant from the NCTE Research Foundation, I sat on the perimeter of the classroom (the way Cindy taught, there was rarely what you'd call the "back" of the room) out among the students. I created on my laptop, as the Terminator would say, "detailed files" of Cindy's teaching and her students' learning. I ended up with nearly 200 pages of single-spaced field notes from these observations, all detailing Cindy's imaginative and dynamic approach to teaching. As I've continued to study Cindy's class over the years with newer generations of doctoral students, they all are blown away by what they see in the field notes as the energy, creativity, thoughtfulness, and accomplishment of Cindy's teaching.

I would be kidding you if I told you that each and every kid in Cindy's class found her teaching to be scintillating each and every day. I taught high school English from 1976–1990, and I know that it just doesn't work that way. One of the problems I have with too much educational writing is that it features success stories only; it seems that any evidence of rough edges, failed experiments, or resistant students reflects negatively on the teacher, as though only the immaculate among us are praiseworthy. When you observe a classroom for a full year, you are thankful that you yourself were never under such scrutiny: You are on display when teaching through an illness, when teaching students who've returned from the smoking area with more than tobacco in their lungs, when trying to reach students whose own parents have given up hope that they'll ever crack open a book. What I found remarkable about Cindy was her incredible patience and optimism when teaching regular kids—the sort that Goodlad (1984) describes as conditioned to the "flat" (p. 108) emotional climate of schools that suggests to them that learning is very dull business indeed.

From my perspective, the classroom of "Ms. O-A," as her students called her, was anything but dull. She worked extraordinarily hard to make the British Literature curriculum engaging for her students. As a teacher, I always avoided the British Literature assignment because I felt that I'd struggle to make the remote language and themes from this canonical body of work interesting and relevant to my students. I always preferred teaching American Literature, which seemed to map so well onto the wakening political interests of high school juniors. Most Brit. Lit. classes of my acquaintance treated the literature as museum pieces to be studied but not touched. To me, that seemingly tactile engagement with literature was a necessary starting point for students in building a meaningful response.

What Cindy did with this class seemed exceptional to me, especially in that she taught in an English department where the prevailing belief was that the curriculum should inculcate students with what the faculty believed to be the Western cultural heritage. The departmental values did not support those weird teachers among us who do not approach the subject according to the resident tradition. My knowledge of Cindy's background helped me to understand why she would not teach in ways that her colleagues found appropriate and students found tedious. Her mother, a kindergarten teacher, had a great influence on her beliefs about teaching, in particular the value of projects, art, activity, interdisciplinary learning, enjoyment, involvement, and other aspects of what we might call engaged learning. At the time I was observing her class, both Cindy's children and mine were enrolled in the same preschool, one that adopted a play-oriented approach to its curriculum. Our kids absolutely loved the school and their teachers. Without question, this orientation to the joy with which young children approach learning based on play and activity—in contrast to the somnambulant experience that too many high school students find their education to be—affected Cindy's decisions about how and what to teach her seniors.

Further, Cindy had begun her teaching career as a speech teacher rather than an English teacher. Many speech classes—and Cindy's were among this group—are very activity-based, with students expected to learn through the process of speaking. There is thus an assumption built in that speech is, to use Barnes's (1991) distinction, *exploratory* more often than it is *final draft*. From this perspective there is great value in talking through half-baked ideas as a way to help them achieve greater cohesion. This premise has influenced such movements as the "writing to learn" approach in which writing is employed to articulate ideas "at the point of utterance" (Applebee 1981, p. 101), rather than serving to state already-developed ideas in final, impeccable form. From her experiences with speech and kindergarten, then, Cindy adopted a teaching approach that involved students in their own learning and appreciated their tentative, provisional efforts at generating ideas through speech and writing—expressive efforts that likely would go through much reconsideration and revision as students explored them with one another. The authenticity of learning in terms of students' real interests was central to Cindy's teaching approach.

I recently read a eulogy to landscape designer Christopher Lloyd, who passed away in early 2006. While the writer's comments refer to Lloyd's philosophy of gardening, it could apply equally well to teaching:

> He taught us to think about gardens and gardening. That gardening should be taken seriously but always in fun and without self-importance or fear. That risks are worth taking, mistakes and failures are inevitable, and tomorrow offers another chance to do something new and better. He encouraged gardeners to live on the "frontier of their experience. . . . It's only those who are afraid of having to admit to mistakes," he wrote, "who are frightened of making them." (Cooper 2006 p. 10)

I found this ethos to be central to Cindy's teaching: Learning was tied to experimental activity in which errors are not only acceptable but often indications that students are stretching their abilities. Under such circumstances, students needn't fear the corrective red pen; they only need to fear complacency and stagnation.

One reason that I chose Cindy's classroom for my research was my interest in what I've called *multimedia composing*—i.e., compositions that may include writing but primarily involve some form of artistic interpretation or expression. Cindy did a terrific job of incorporating the arts into her English instruction. In addition to the body biographies that Cindy and I have written about (O'Donnell-Allen and Smagorinsky 1999; Smagorinsky and O'Donnell-Allen 1998a, 1998b, 2000), her students produced masks representing their identities (Smagorinsky, Zoss, and O'Donnell-Allen 2005), frequently used art as an interpretive medium, incorporated aspects of drama into routine literature instruction, and in general engaged with the curriculum through active, multimodal means. While some students always wondered why the other English teachers were so different from Cindy, and why they weren't always reading the same things, many were glad to be in a classroom in which literary study came to life in surprising and illuminating ways.

Another quality that distinguished Cindy's teaching was her dedication to scaffolding students' learning. Cindy was willing to invest quite a bit of instructional time in preparing students for the work she expected of them. In the great "breadth vs. depth" debate, she came down squarely on the side of depth. I'll give one seemingly innocuous illustration of some teaching she did early in the year. She wanted the students to maintain double-entry reading logs; i.e., logs divided into two columns, with provocative quotes on one side and commentary or exploratory writing of some sort on the other. Now, assigning students such a log might appear on the surface to be simple; just give the instructions and just about anybody ought to be able to follow them. Cindy never made the assumption that students could simply do what she told them to do. Rather, she meticulously prepared the students for this task.

She prepared a handout that described her expectations for the reading logs, including illustrations of 20 different types of responses, which she reviewed with the students in class; in addition, she wrote instructions on the chalkboard for how to produce reading log entries. She then had students work in small groups to produce a collaborative reading log entry, using an accessible poem related to the unit theme (identity) to stimulate their thinking. When they were done, she went systematically through each group, reconstructing their log responses on the board and leading the class in a brief discussion and critique of each. Only when she was certain that everyone grasped the nature of the task and why she was assigning it did Cindy move to the independent stage of the sequence: For homework, each student was to write one double-entry reading log response on another poem that she provided. After her assessment of these efforts, Cindy was finally confident that her students were prepared to maintain more extensive logs on their own.

Most teachers I know do not invest this amount of time in teaching students *how to do* the tasks that they assign. I greatly admired Cindy's dedication of instructional time to learning processes, typically at the expense of content coverage. Senior English classes more commonly cover the whole range of anthologized British literature, "from Beowulf to Virginia Woolf," moving through the bewildering language and archaic topics with little attention to how teenagers might process them. Cindy was far more interested in ensuring that her students learned what they studied, and learned new ways of studying it, rather than taking the more typical approach of explaining the arcana of centuries-old literature in lectures and then testing students on their recall of this critically accepted wisdom.

One student in this class, referred to in our publications as "Jay," made the following observation during one of my interviews with him:

Jay: My normal English experiences are you come in and you do the work. You do their writings they want you to and you have homework and you really don't know the teacher at all. There's no personal level. You just come in and you do it and leave and that's all you take with you. But here, I think you're just going to have a lot more memories—something I can take with me in a real way.

PS: What's not memorable about what you're accustomed to?

Jay: You don't remember every paper you wrote. I mean you remember the big ones, but I mean you go day-to-day and you write like this—you answer the questions and that doesn't really relate to your life at all. You won't remember that. That has no importance at the time. I mean it's a grade and that's all it is. Here we're getting something that's—we can tell our kids that we did—tell our friends—something that's interesting.

This quality of being memorable is something I've often talked about in my English education classes. I ask students about their most memorable experiences as students in their high school education. For the most part, their high school days—at least those concerned with academics—are not very memorable at all. My students have a general memory of sitting in classes being bored because the teaching is talking and no one is listening. What they do find memorable—and therefore important, I believe—are those occasions when they *did* something: went somewhere interesting, worked on a project with friends, wrote and performed a play, and so on. Jay's comments distill for me what made Cindy's class so outstanding: Her students believed that they would carry memories of it well into adulthood. This impact, I think, is not due to her innate charisma, but rather to her careful, thoughtful approach to teaching that helped to produce such memorable occasions and important products.

*The Book Club Companion: Fostering Strategic Readers in the Secondary Classroom* is the book that I've always hoped Cindy would write. In it she shares activities she developed to help engage teenagers with the high school English curriculum. I've seen her implement these strategies and can testify that most of her students used these activities in thoughtful and productive ways. *The Book Club Companion* also illustrates what it takes to teach as a reflective practitioner. After examining the teacher research group she formed at OU, Cindy contends that, given the limited value of most of what passes for inservice education, schools would do well to promote collaborative teacher inquiry as its primary inservice vehicle. *The Book Club Companion* is a testament to what is possible when teachers think carefully about what they do. What we have here is not simply a guidebook to effective practice, but an experience in reflective practice. I hope that you find *The Book Club Companion* as powerful and provocative as I do.

—Peter Smagorinsky

## References

Applebee, A. N. 1981. *Writing in the Secondary School: English and the Content Areas*. Urbana, IL: National Council of Teachers of English.

Barnes, D. 1991. *From Communication to Curriculum*. 2 ed. Portsmouth, NH: Heinemann.

Cooper, T. C. 2006. "Christopher Lloyd, March 2, 1921–January 27, 2006." *Horticulture* 103(4): 10.

Goodlad, J. I. 1984. *A Place Called School: Prospects for the Future*. New York: McGraw-Hill.

O'Donnell-Allen, C. 2001. "Teaching with a Questioning Mind: The Development of a Teacher Research Group into a Discourse Community." *Research in the Teaching of English* 36: 161–211.

O'Donnell-Allen, C., and P. Smagorinsky. 1999. "Revising Ophelia: Rethinking Questions of Gender and Power in School." *English Journal* 88(3): 35–42.

Smagorinsky, P. 1997. "Personal Growth in Social Context: A High School Senior's Search for Meaning in and Through Writing." *Written Communication* 14: 63–105.

Smagorinsky, P., and C. O'Donnell-Allen. 1998a. "The Depth and Dynamics of Context: Tracing the Sources and Channels of Engagement and Disengagement in Students' Response to Literature." *Journal of Literacy Research* 30: 515–59.

Smagorinsky, P., and C. O'Donnell-Allen. 1998b. "Reading as Mediated and Mediating Action: Composing Meaning for Literature Through Multimedia Interpretive Texts." *Reading Research Quarterly* 33: 198–226.

Smagorinsky, P., and C. O'Donnell-Allen. 2000. "Idiocultural Diversity in Small Groups: The Role of the Relational Framework in Collaborative Learning." In *Vygotskian Perspectives on Literacy Research: Constructing Meaning Through Collaborative Inquiry*, ed. C. D. Lee and P. Smagorinsky; 165–90. New York: Cambridge University Press.

Smagorinsky, P., M. Zoss, and C. O'Donnell-Allen. 2005. "Mask-Making as Identity Project in a High School English Class: A Case Study." *English in Education* 39(2): 58–73.

# Acknowledgments

I wrote much of this manuscript while sitting in a small-town coffee shop, and one day the counter guy said, "See that guy over there? That guy is writing a book. Can you believe that? I can't believe that. Now that's some high standards." I thought about telling him that I was writing one, too, but then I thought again.

Because do you know what people do when you tell them you are writing a book? They look at you like you are set apart or at least you *think* you are or, even worse, maybe you should be. Especially people who know you. Their eyes tend to squint or widen. Some people even wince a little as if you've surely lost your ever-lovin' mind or have gotten too big for your britches. When this happened to me, I tried not to take it personally.

But there were a few people who actually smiled when I mumbled my intentions, and to them I owe my eternal thanks. Thank you, first of all, to the strong women in my life! My friend and colleague Louann Reid convinced me one summer afternoon that it was time to write this book and then in her typical fashion made it seem as if this was something I could actually do. Jenny Goodman, who read and responded to earlier drafts of this work, should really think about taking up cheerleading, though the uniform might conflict with her feminist sensibilities. Pam Coke and my other colleagues in the English department at Colorado State University continue to support my work even though the honeymoon period should be long gone by now. Finally, Sonja Chapman ushered me through the production process with warmth and efficiency.

Now on to the men. Peter Smagorinsky may be wondering when his gig with me will be up. (He probably should read up on *imprinting*.) Peter has been my mentor ever since he talked me into a graduate program in 1991. His work continues to inspire me as much intellectually as his encouragement does professionally. My editor, Jim Strickland, doesn't realize it yet, but he, too, has signed on for life. Had it not been for his steady encouragement and thoughtful response, this book would not be in your hands.

Thanks also to the writing project folks at Colorado State University and the University of Oklahoma, my friends at Norman High School, and all the students who have contributed to this project. Your continuing presence in my life reminds me why I still love my job. Thanks especially to Rebecca Fox, Stan McReynolds, and other teachers and students from Poudre School District who have opened their classrooms to book clubs.

I also want to thank my friends who remembered to ask me how the writing was going and reassured me I could do this regardless of my answer. Thanks, too, to the fine folks at Saxby's, who never failed to deliver smiles along with endless cups of tea. But thanks most of all to my dear family, who consumed a lot of pizza, ignored the cobwebs, and stepped over even bigger than usual piles of books while I was writing this. Will, Lexie, Lynley, and Austen, you bring love, light, and laughter into every day of my life.

# Introduction: Welcome to the Book Club

Even if you don't use book clubs in your classroom yet, you're probably already familiar with the concept. Who isn't these days? Entire cities are reading the same book, encouraging their citizens to get in small groups and talk it over, and inviting the author in for lectures at the end. Oprah has revived her book club, and authors and publishers compete to secure her branding, a guarantee that the book will be a bestseller, among women at least. A 2006 Google search turned up about 125 million hits for *book clubs* as a search term, and books for all ages are now routinely published with book club discussion questions in the back.

Perhaps the true measure of their ubiquity, however, came on Valentine's Day 2003 in a most unlikely place, a box of Conversation Hearts. I had been delighted when *EMAIL ME* and *FAX ME* appeared, but even I didn't expect the debut of, you guessed it, *BOOK CLUB*. What further evidence do we need that book clubs have truly gone mainstream?

I started using a version of book clubs with my high school English students more than fifteen years ago, but in 2000, when I started matching college preservice teachers up with kids to form book clubs in secondary schools, I discovered that few professional resources existed to guide our work. All of the teachers with whom we were working had heard of book clubs, but they weren't sure how to implement them in the classroom. Some of the teachers had also heard of *literature circles*, and they wondered aloud, were book clubs the same thing? Not really, I'd explain, but at the time, the only book I knew to recommend was *The Book Club Connection* (McMahon and Raphael 1997), and as wonderful as this book is, it focuses primarily on elementary classrooms.

As a result, I found myself scrambling to help teachers understand how book clubs can also work in the secondary classroom. I told more stories than I knew I remembered about how book clubs worked in my high school classroom. I dug up all the book club materials I'd generated over the years, created new resources for the classrooms I was working with at the time, and stored everything in manila files. As the number of classrooms expanded, and the files turned into piles, I discovered there wasn't enough of me to go around. That's when my friend and colleague Louann Reid advised me that it was time to write this book.

The very next day I started making a list of the questions that teachers new to book clubs regularly asked me and the things I wished I'd known about book clubs before I began using them. These items fell into the following categories, which eventually shaped the organization of this book:

⚙ *Definitions.* In order to grasp the extraordinary flexibility of book clubs, I reasoned that you'd need to know how book clubs differ from reading groups, small-group discussions, and literature circles. In other words, because these other contexts are so familiar, you'd probably need to understand what book clubs *aren't* in order to understand what they really are. I tackle definitions in Chapter 1.

⚙ *The Bottom Line.* Every teacher I know wonders, "How can I help my students become more willing, engaged, and strategic readers?" I figured you'd like to know what theory and research say about adolescent readers' needs so that you'd better understand how book clubs can help meet them. I synthesize this professional literature in Chapter 2.

⚙ *The Lay of the Land.* Regardless of how well book clubs should work in theory, I knew you'd want to see how they really play out in actual classrooms. How did I get started using book clubs? How did my students respond? What worked and what didn't, and what questions emerged along the way? What changes have I made, and why? In Chapter 3, I invite you into my classroom to see how teacher research has informed my book club journey over the past fifteen years.

⚙ *Getting Organized.* We all know that even the best practices can fall flat if we and our students aren't adequately prepared to make use of them, so I suspect you'd like some ground rules and suggestions for setting up book clubs so that they will run as smoothly as possible from the start. In Chapter 4, I discuss the curricular, instructional, and procedural aspects of book club preparation, such as integrating book clubs into your curriculum, assessing students' needs, choosing books, and organizing students into groups.

◈ *Getting Going.* I also knew you'd want to see the materials I've developed to help students prepare for and sustain substantive book club discussions. In Chapter 5, you'll find lots of response tools designed to prompt their conversations, tools for keeping track of the discussions, and suggestions for what to do with yourself while students are doing all the talking.

◈ *Assessment.* Regardless of how authentic book clubs might be in approximating the real-life experiences of readers outside of school, I knew you'd need resources for assessing students along the way and at the end of the line. Chapter 6 discusses principles for book club assessment and includes several suggestions for culminating projects and how to evaluate them.

◈ *Resources.* Finally, in the appendices, I recommend several book sets, organized by grade level and key concepts, and provide resources for curriculum planning. I also include reproducible masters and scoring guides for the strategies mentioned throughout the book.

In various configurations, book clubs have been a part of American culture for longer than you might imagine (for an abbreviated history, see Faust et al. 2005). Yet at the moment, the world outside of schools has made something as simple as reading books and talking about them in small groups seem contemporary, hip even. *The Book Club Companion* is meant to help you and your students ride this particular cultural tide. It's the book I wished for fifteen years ago as a high school teacher, the one that the secondary teachers I know now are looking for but none of us can find. I hope it will grant you and your students lifetime membership to the book club.

# The Book Club Companion

# What Is a Book Club Anyway?

ook clubs have been a staple in my classroom for more than fifteen years, though I wasn't calling them that in the beginning. As I explain in Chapter 3, book clubs started out as "novel workshops" in my classroom, and it was only the rising popularity of the term *book club* in mainstream culture, coupled with my exposure to *The Book Club Connection* (McMahon and Raphael 1997), that made me rethink the name. I have learned that book clubs hold great potential for meeting the needs of a wide range of adolescent readers, but when I tell other secondary teachers about them, the first question they inevitably ask goes something like this: "What's the difference between book clubs and old-fashioned reading groups or literature circles?"

My all-purpose answer is that book clubs are *small groups of readers that meet on a regular basis to systematically discuss books (and other texts) of the members' choice. These groups use a variety of response methods to prompt and extend book club discussion, and membership varies according to the desired configuration.* In other words, the key feature of book clubs is *flexibility*.

Let me flesh out this definition one key concept at a time:

**1.** *Book clubs are made up of small groups of readers.* I've found the optimum size of book clubs to be four to six readers. Though it's possible to meet in a trio, one absent member puts an undue onus on those who remain when the club suddenly becomes a couple. Couples often gravitate to one or the other end of the spectrum of conflict versus complementarity. Since one of the great benefits of book clubs is exploring the diversity of individual members' responses to texts, and pairs tend to minimize that diversity, starting off with three members is a risk that will almost surely result in pairs of readers and a corresponding lack of diversity at some point. Book clubs exceeding the number of six are also problematic but for the opposite reason. In a group this large, the responses of individuals tend to be obscured. When one can get lost in the crowd, so can the benefits of small-group discourse, namely the intellectual stretching that comes as a result of holding one's ideas up against others'.

**2.** *Book clubs meet on a regular basis.* In working with readers from middle school through graduate school, I've found that with secondary students, weekly meetings have proved optimal. Book clubs need to meet often enough to maintain momentum yet not so often as to prevent time for reading and independent mulling over of ideas.

Television series play weekly for a reason. A week is just long enough to look forward to the next episode without forgetting or tiring of the plot. Book clubs are much the same way. When students meet less frequently than once a week, they are likely to have trouble maintaining collaborative memory or momentum. They may lose track of key plot developments or forget where the group left off conceptually last time. And they're unlikely to develop an ongoing set of key questions or themes that crop up repeatedly in the text. Even when students have completed individual written responses, they may forget the detail that made the response seem so important at the time and thus be less likely to offer it up for the group's consideration. It would be a shame to rob book clubs of the chance to act as a testing ground.

Yet meeting too frequently is also problematic. Kids are busy, busy, busy, and when book clubs meet twice or more a week, students often don't have time to complete a good chunk of independent reading. And prepare a substantive response. And go to hockey practice. And wash the dishes. And check their email. And so on. The kind of reflective reading made possible by book clubs also takes time. I recently had the pleasure of hosting my high school daughter's book club on *East of Eden*. Students would often open their weekly meetings with the phrase "Well, I've been thinking a lot this week about . . . ," and they would fill in the blank with everything from the significance of biblical allusions to the origins of good and evil. *East of Eden* is a tough book for most adults, much less fifteen-year-olds, and had the group met daily, I'm doubtful they would have had time to mull over their ideas long enough to synthesize them into more significant conclusions.

When students meet less or more than once a week, book clubs can fail either way. When students have forgotten why they're meeting in the first place or they aren't meaningfully prepared to participate, conversations are superficial at best, and their minds and, soon, their behaviors begin to wander. Additionally, on the days in between book club meetings, teachers have the opportunity to teach new reading strategies and thematically related shorter texts or make time for related projects, writing workshops, and independent reading.

**3.** *Book clubs engage in systematic discussion.* In my first few years of using book clubs, which I describe in detail in Chapter 3, I found that individual book clubs inevitably establish their own routines, but students appreciate a system that outlines the before, during, and after. In other words, they want to know how to prepare for book club, what will happen when they get there, and what will come after they've finished the book, as far as final projects and evaluation go. In terms of what happens *during* book club, discussions are at least initially prompted by the individual responses students make to the books they're reading between weekly meetings. Even though students identify the topics worth talking about, they need structured support in keeping track of these individual responses, and they also need advance notice of how these responses will come into play during meetings. I have discovered the hard way that you can't simply ask students to read their individual responses and expect that a magical discussion will ensue. In fact, more often than not, this approach typically results in recitations followed by a whole lot of dead air. So how *do* you get kids to make meaningful conversation about books?

You provide a road map of sorts—one that offers enough direction so they won't wander aimlessly and they can keep track of where they're going but that also allows for freedom in selecting from among the multiple roads to Rome. As much as we'd like for it to be true, all students don't grow up in households where books are read and discussed on a regular basis the way they are in book clubs. This doesn't mean students don't read and discuss other texts outside of our classrooms or hear and tell stories again and again within their families. But we're asking them to talk about specific texts (usually literary) in specific ways (usually rooted in literary theories and literacy research) in a specific context (our English classrooms). We have to help them learn, rather than expect them to come to us already knowing, the system that I discuss for the rest of this book.

**4.** *Book clubs discuss books (and other texts) of the members' choice.* Book clubs work best when kids get to choose the books. This means that different book clubs are reading different books all at the same time. If you choose one book for everyone in the class to read, don't expect that students will have the literary experience of a lifetime simply because you've put them in small groups, or pseudo book clubs, to discuss it. Why not just teach the book to the entire class in this case?

At least since Dewey, educators have known that curiosity and learning go hand in hand, yet students rarely have a say in what they get taught in school. Book clubs provide a natural opportunity for them to do so and to grow as readers in the process. Why? Because choice allows students to discover and develop their own reader identities. Choice creates ownership because students have a real say in crafting the curriculum. But most importantly, choice increases the likelihood of buy-in, which increases motivation to read.

Of course, even in book clubs, choices are usually limited by external constraints, such as book budgets, curricular expectations, developmental appropriateness, community sensibilities, and so forth. To meet these constraints in my high school classroom, I selected five to six books that were varied enough to appeal to a wide range of kids yet had enough in common to cohere around a particular theme, say rebels, trailblazers, and scapegoats. Then I offered a brief book talk on each book and asked kids to list for me their top three choices. From there, I sorted the votes and adjusted the groups so that each book club had four to six reasonably compatible members. I use this method to this day because it has been fail-safe in ensuring students one of their top three choices.

**5.** *Book clubs use a variety of open-ended response methods to prompt and extend book club discussion.* Because book clubs are flexible enough to incorporate a range of instructional strategies, they can be tailored to meet various constellations of reader needs and preferences, teacher objectives, and instructional standards. Consider, for instance, a group of seventh graders with whom I worked in Stan McReynolds's English class. This all-boy book club was highly motivated to read Art Spiegelman's *Maus*, reluctant to write about it, but willing to respond with sketches in kind. Stan and I wanted their responses to prompt book club discussion about the most significant events in the book up to this point. Grade-level standards required the development of prediction strategies, but since visual responses would be insufficient preparation for their upcoming standardized tests, we knew it was also important that students write.

Consequently, we asked students to create visual reading logs in preparation for book club (Note: All response tools mentioned in this and subsequent chapters are included in Appendix C). The log, which we named 1-2-3-Predict, consisted of four rectangles. In the first three rectangles, students drew the three most important events in the section of the book they'd just read. In the space under each of these rectangles, students wrote a caption explaining the significance of the illustrated event. In the fourth rectangle, students sketched a scene predicting what they thought might happen in the next section of the book. The caption under this rectangle explained why this event was likely to occur.

These reading logs appealed to students because they were allowed to draw. The logs worked for Stan and me because students were required to make interpretive decisions about the text's most important events that would likely encourage meaningful book club discussion, especially when students chose different events. The logs also met standards surrounding the skills of prediction and inference because they supplied a visualization strategy students could use later in the book and with other texts as well. Finally, the logs gave students practice in justifying their interpretations through writing, the medium preferred on standardized tests.

In using book clubs with eleventh graders in my honors English class, students' needs, my objectives, and instructional standards were vastly different from those that guided my work with Stan's seventh graders. Thus the response tools varied as well. As I describe in Chapter 3, students wrote Real Books Letters in preparation for book clubs, used book club discussion records to keep track of their responses, and produced readers' theatre scripts and analytical essays as final projects. The constants in both settings, however, were the open-ended nature of the response strategies and, of course, the book club setting itself.

**6.** *Book club membership varies according to the desired configuration.* Book clubs typically are made up only of same-aged students, but they sometimes include a teacher or more able peer as well. In my high school classroom, book clubs are made up only of students enrolled in the class. While students meet, I browse around the room, making observational notes, eavesdropping on book club conversations, and sometimes sitting in, but only for a few moments. In this case, I provide considerable front-loading so that students understand my expectations, book club logistics, and culminating assessments before they go it alone.

When possible or desirable, however, book clubs can also benefit from the presence of a teacher or classroom volunteer such as a parent, grandparent, or older student. Again, substantial front-loading is required but this time for the purpose of helping volunteers understand that their goal is to help students become more independent readers by facilitating rather than dominating book club discussion. These volunteers can act as mentors, increasing student motivation for reading and modeling the interpretive processes engaged readers typically use. While I don't recommend ability grouping in book clubs, mentors can benefit readers at every developmental level by providing extra support for struggling readers and enrichment for highly motivated and advanced readers.

## Distinguishing Book Clubs from Reading Groups, Small-Group Discussions, and Literature Circles

Obviously, I'm not the first person to suggest that discussing books in small groups is a good idea. But the small groups I've just described are not identical to other familiar configurations like reading groups complete with round-robin reading, small-group discussions, and literature circles. In the following sections, I explain some of the differences.

### How Book Clubs Differ from Reading Groups

Even we secondary teachers are probably familiar with traditional reading groups where an elementary teacher sits in the curve of a kidney-shaped table and listens to children read aloud, round-robin style, from short texts. Assigned by the teacher, these short texts, usually found in basal readers, contain controlled vocabulary at students' developmental reading level. The discourse in reading groups is typically controlled as well. While students take turns reading, the teacher corrects or helps with pronunciation and then asks questions intended to check students' comprehension of literal details found in the passage. Aside from their size and regular meeting times, reading groups bear no other resemblance to book clubs because they do not allow students to choose texts, use a variety of response tools, or participate in discussion aimed at extended interpretation. In fact, as Bernice Cullinan notes in her introduction to *The Book Club Connection* (1997), although student participation seems to be central in traditional reading groups, these groups are actually teacher centered since teachers get to make all the important decisions and also do most of the talking.

Even though teacher-led reading groups are more commonplace in elementary classrooms than in secondary ones, the primary method used in these groups, that is, round-robin reading, is still a staple in many English classrooms, especially when teachers want students to focus simultaneously on a lengthy text, such as a play, a book chapter, or a longish short story. Round-robin reading *feels* right because it's so familiar. The practice does seem democratic because everyone takes a turn, and it appears unifying because everyone is ostensibly on the same page. Yet such reading might more accurately be referred to as recitation.

Since at least 1979 (True), round-robin reading hasn't been recommended for several reasons. First of all, less capable readers can find the performance element present in reading groups to be nerve-racking and sometimes embarrassing, and their reading is sometimes difficult to follow when pronunciation or comprehension difficulties disrupt the pace of the story. Even though these readers do need more practice, reading aloud in front of their peers isn't the best way for them to get it. Beers (2003) recommends buddy reading or guided reading as good alternatives that help adolescent readers achieve reading fluency.

Second, if a text is appropriate for students to read aloud, they should be able to read it independently. If the text is too difficult for students to read for themselves but is still appropriate to their interests, then this text would be a good choice for the teacher to read to the entire class. Also, during round-robin reading, the students who aren't reading are often unfocused on the text for the majority of the time and catch up right before their turn arrives. Students have perfected this technique. Once when I was observing a student teacher who had asked students to read *Romeo and Juliet* in this manner, I saw students passing notes, filing their nails, completing homework for other classes, in short, doing anything *but* engaging with the text while they waited for their turn to read. Because round-robin reading can be tedious, students can easily lose interest in the text.

So why are reading groups and round-robin reading still so common? Because they are as familiar to teachers as grammar workbooks and spelling tests on Fridays, and old traditions die hard. Remembering that these exercises didn't hurt us as students, reasoning that we turned out all right, and unaware of better alternatives, we sometimes just teach as we were taught. Yet even able, fluent adult readers often have difficulty recalling details of a text during round-robin reading because they are so focused on the performance aspect of reading aloud. In other words, good intentions not withstanding, traditional reading groups that feature round-robin reading can actually *inhibit* students from engaging with texts and constructing meaning with one another.

That's why most of the reading students do for book clubs actually takes place silently prior to the book club meeting, either for homework or during independent reading time in class. Of course students often read passages aloud to the rest of the group during book club discussions. The difference is they do so by choice and in the service of interpretation, usually to bolster a claim they're making in a student-centered conversation.

## How Book Clubs Differ from Small-Group Discussions

Back in 1985, the buzzword was *cooperative learning*. I still believe that small groups are especially effective contexts for literature discussions, but I don't believe small-group discussions of literature are necessarily akin to book clubs. That's because the tasks these small groups are asked to complete are often teacher centered. Let me illustrate with an example from my first few years of teaching.

In my undergraduate methods class, we pored over poems and short stories and designed small-group discussion questions based on George Hillocks' (1980) well-known hierarchy that ranks questions according to how they gauge different levels of comprehension, from literal to inferential. As I understood it then, my job as an English teacher was to read a text as closely as I could, squeeze out all its meaning, and then design questions along this hierarchy for the purpose of leading my students toward the same—need I even say it, "sophisticated"—interpretation I had reached. Students would meet in small groups to answer these study questions, as I called them, and in the process would grasp all that was essential about the text, absorbing from my example what it meant to ask important questions about literature.

Only, when I eagerly tried my questions out on my students, this didn't actually happen. True, classes were predictable, and students were mostly dutiful, but all of us were bored stiff. Were students in small groups? Yes. Were they discussing books? Yes. Weren't these book clubs, then? No, because even though I wasn't actually sitting in on the groups, I might as well have been. They were as teacher centered as it gets.

I wasn't surprised at the conclusions students reached because I'd confined their so-called inquiry as carefully as a Hot Wheels car to my own interpretive track. Their chief concern was getting the right answer—read, *my* answer—because they never got to pose any questions of their own. And because I never asked them to reflect on the nature of the questions I was asking, they didn't learn strategies for doing so. In fact, I was the one using all the strategies because I was the one asking all the questions.

In book clubs, students still use teacher-designed response tools, but these are far more open-ended, demanding that students make independent interpretive choices and develop awareness of the strategies they're implementing so they can transfer these to future texts. Because these individual responses are then used to fuel book club discussions, and individuals seldom see one text one way, students are more inclined to question and challenge, to augment and extend—in other words, to construct meaning together.

## How Book Clubs Differ from Literature Circles

Harvey Daniels deserves most of the credit for making literature circles the classroom version of a household term. In the second edition of *Literature Circles: Voice and Choice in Book Clubs and Reading Groups*, Daniels (2002) uses the terms *reading groups*, *book clubs*, and *literature circles* interchangeably and defines them as "student-led small-group book discussions" (18). Sounds a lot like my definition of book clubs, right?

Well, yes and no. And that's probably because I was using book clubs in my classroom for several years before I even knew that literature circles existed. This is neither good nor bad, but simply so. Some of the features of literature circles that Daniels emphasizes are also common to my definition of book clubs—namely, small-group contexts, routine scheduling, and student choice in texts and topics. Before I begin enumerating the differences between literature circles and book clubs, however, I want to be very clear. In doing so, *I am not arguing that literature circles ought to be abandoned because book clubs are the only way*. If I did so, I would be negating a method that many teachers value as indispensable in their classrooms. Rather, I want to describe some of the *logistical differences* between the two and explain how they are informed by *different principles for literary response and small-group learning* that result in *curricular flexibility*.

**LOGISTICAL DIFFERENCES** The first difference has to do with book club duration and membership. Daniels (2002) stresses that literature circles are temporary and task based: "Once they have finished their job—reading and discussing a book of common interest—the group disbands and individual members find their way into new, different groups by picking their next book" (19). Certainly this can be, and has been, the case in my classroom. But sometimes, a book club works so hard to build a context distinguished by equal degrees of challenge and support that they understandably want to stay together. Like many adult book clubs I know, such groups privilege the relationship they've formed over the book they've read.

Take my friend Jane, for example, whose daughter plays on my daughter's soccer team. Jane comes to many soccer games with book in hand, reading up for her adult book club during warm-ups and half-time, and I'm always there to ask, "Whatcha reading? Is it any good?" More than once, I've been surprised by her answer. The last time Jane confessed that she didn't really like the book, I had to ask why she continued with the book club.

"Oh, honey," she said, "it's not about the books, it's about the company." She went on to explain that members took turns suggesting books, and her turn would roll around again soon. In the meantime, she was willing to read books that weren't necessarily her favorites because of the great respect she had for the other members of her book club. She trusted that if one of the terrific human beings in her book club chose the book, something about it was worthwhile, so she was willing to keep on reading and have her mind changed by the conversation. For Jane, the intellectual rewards of book clubs walk hand in hand with the social.

I've seen the same thing happen with adolescent readers who've chosen to stay together for more than one round of book club. As long as a book club is functioning well socially and staying on task, I tell them to go for it. Far be it from me to disrupt what's working well with adolescent readers! When the group is ready for a new book, the members consider the available choices and make a selection by consensus.

A second difference between the book clubs I describe here and the literature circles described by Daniels is that he stresses that discussion topics in literature circles come only from students. This is mostly the case in book clubs as well, but the Book Club Discussion Records featured in Chapter 5 provide a good example of how teachers can also offer topics in order to maintain continuity among book clubs but still avoid dominating discussion.

The text clusters students read during book club segments in my classroom are usually related by theme, genre, or project. For instance, in a thematic unit on personal choice and social justice, tenth graders might choose from *Catalyst*, *Holes*, *Monster*, *To Kill a Mockingbird*, and *Bless Me, Ultima*. After recording and discussing their own topics and questions on a discussion record, students conclude the book club session by considering one question I've provided that is thematically relevant to all the books. This question reinforces important aspects of the unit or allows me to push the group's thinking in ways they might not have considered, and it also ensures a common thread for all the book clubs. If class time permits after book clubs have concluded for a particular day, groups sometimes briefly report their answers to the common question to the rest of the class. Hearing what others have said extends discussion of the unit theme, familiarizes groups with one another's books, and often generates interest in the books others are reading as well.

**THEORETICAL FLEXIBILITY OF BOOK CLUBS** Another aspect that distinguishes literature circles from book clubs stems less from logistics. By design, the literary theory informing literature circles is reader response theory (e.g., Rosenblatt 1938, 1978). Daniels (2002) explains that in literature circles, "the base for everything is 'just reading' and 'just responding' to lots and lots of books" (23). The featured response tool in doing so is the "role sheet," though Daniels also discusses a handful of other tools. In preparation for literature circles, students take on different roles (e.g., connector, questioner, literary luminary, illustrator, etc.). These roles require students to employ various strategies proficient readers use and are delineated by open-ended prompts on their respective role sheets. For instance, the "connector" notes "connections [he] made between this reading and [his] own experiences, the wider world, and other texts or authors" (107). Students use these comments to channel book club discussions, and they rotate roles in the course of the literature circle.

Book clubs, too, draw on reader response theory in that they enable students to generate and share their personal responses to books, but again, the key feature of book clubs is flexibility. As you will see in the chapters that follow, book clubs draw on other literary theories in addition to reader response and emphasize a wider range of response tools than role sheets. This feature, probably more than any other, distinguishes book clubs from literature circles.

**COLLABORATIVE LEARNING AND CURRICULAR FLEXIBILITY IN BOOK CLUBS** Although the computer on which I'm writing suggests that *cooperation* and *collaboration* are synonyms, these words actually have different meanings when applied to small-group learning (Damon and Phelps 1989; John-Steiner 2000). Vera John-Steiner explains that "participants in cooperative endeavors each make specific contributions to a shared task. However, their level of involvement may differ, as well as their sense of intellectual ownership of the resulting product" (12). Literature circles provide a good example of *cooperative learning* in the way role sheets are designed to prompt students' written response and discussion by "giving kids clearly defined, interlocking, and open-ended tasks" (13). In other words, each role is meant to constitute a different piece of an idealized reader's cognitive puzzle. Thus, literature circles divide up the cognitive labor of reading, as each member takes up just one piece of the puzzle and fits it together with other members' pieces to complete the reading experience. The goal is that by trying every role on for size in the course of a literature circle, students will eventually internalize all of them.

One of the drawbacks of cooperative learning, however, is that while it completes the puzzle, the pieces don't necessarily have to interact in the process. Rather, they can easily remain discrete parts of a whole. If I stick to my role and you stick to yours, we can still cooperate to complete the task without ever truly influencing one another. Daniels (2002) reports that the same can happen in literature circles when students misuse role sheets as ends in and of themselves. Literature circle discussions can devolve into mere reporting if "kids just go around the circle, reading their role sheets one after the other, and never get into a real conversation" (13). For that reason, Daniels emphasizes that role sheets ought to be temporary supports, and he suggests alternative methods for encouraging interaction in literature circles in the second edition of *Literature Circles* (see also *Mini-Lessons for Literature Circles* [2005], coauthored by Daniels and Nancy Steineke). Unfortunately, the literature circles I observe and hear secondary teachers describe often feature a steady diet of role sheets, even after several rounds.

Don't get me wrong: If I'd have known that literature circles existed when I started using book clubs in my classroom, I'd no doubt have tried role sheets. The puzzle metaphor just seems so darn logical. Yet research based on think-aloud protocols, in which readers describe their reading processes while they're reading, reveals that even experienced readers' processes are by no means logical or linear (see, for instance, Wolf 1988). Rather, they are recursive, full of stops and starts and missteps as readers lunge forward and circle back, revising their initial interpretations as connections pop into their heads or new information comes along. Thus even the individual reader's cognitive puzzle pieces are less discrete than logic might suggest. For instance, the reader doesn't "define new words" first before "making personal connections" or "posing questions." Rather, these processes mingle fluidly, influencing one another in unpredictable ways to produce interpretations that are provisional at best.

Book clubs, on the other hand, are based on a *collaborative model for learning*, the premise being that if processes within the individual reader are so dynamic, then we need to find similarly dynamic ways of encouraging interactions *among* readers. John-Steiner (2000) explains that collaborative learning is characterized by a "fully realized equality in roles and responsibilities" because participants "see themselves engaged in a joint task" (13, emphasis mine). In book clubs, the joint task is to build an interpretation of a text together through exploratory acts of composing, including writing, visualizing, and speaking.

To develop the myriad habits of mind practiced by engaged readers, book clubs rely on curricular flexibility. Depending on readers' needs and teachers' instructional goals, students use a wide variety of response tools instead of relying on just one. While their individual responses do foster book club discussion, students aren't confined to a single role. Book club discussions tend to be free-flowing as a result. My thought may end where yours begins, and because our roles aren't hard-and-fast, you may make a connection or pose a question I hadn't considered. I may in turn extend your idea toward a new conclusion so that both of our interpretations are stretched ever after.

Thus, while in literature circles, each member's individual puzzle piece (i.e., role sheet) is still recognizable in the end product, in book clubs, ideas and functions mingle so completely that no one can take sole credit for the final outcome. Though each book club member clearly contributes, tracing an individual's discrete contribution is almost as impossible as identifying the single shade of blue in an impressionistic painting. Further support for a collaborative approach is provided by the research conducted by Donna Alvermann and her colleagues (1996), who found that open-ended tasks that require group collaboration, as opposed to division of labor among individuals, are an essential component of effective discussion in small groups. Over time, then, the sum can become greater than the whole of its parts. In Chapters 4 and 5, I describe how to set book clubs up to support this kind of collaborative learning.

## Recognizing a Book Club If You Saw One

So if you stepped into my classroom, how would you distinguish a book club from a reading group, a small-group discussion, or a literature circle? About once a week, you would see small groups of four to six students discussing topics of their choice drawn from books of their choice as the teacher browsed around the room among groups. Students wouldn't take turns reading around the circle, but sometimes, in the midst of discussion, a student might flip through the book and read a passage aloud as she made a large point or reminded her peers of a significant event that occurred in the portion of the book they had read independently prior to book club.

Over time, you'd see that the membership in some book clubs remained the same while other kids switched from group to group depending on their reading preferences. You'd note the absence of teacher-prepared study questions and see that the response tools students used to prompt their conversations depended on the instructional purpose, student need, and/or featured literary theory at the time. In one book club, you might hear a student drawing attention to images from the Mind Map he drew for the narrator from Poe's "The Telltale Heart." Another day, you might see a student reading from her Real Books Letter about the personal connections she'd made to Cather's *My Antonia*. In another book club, a student might refer to Internet research he'd conducted on censorship as the group discussed Lasky's *Memoirs of a Bookbat*. And in yet another book club, you might see a student identifying race, class, and gender distinctions in a scene from Porter's *Imani All Mine* as prompted by her Sticky Notes Bookmark.

You'd see collaborative conversation as opposed to cooperative reporting out, and someone would be keeping track of the conversation using a Book Club Discussion Record so that the group could reflect on their responses later and synthesize them in a culminating project after they had finished the book. In short, even though each group would be discussing a different book and the topics would obviously vary, even though the response tools might change from week to week, the conversation would be purposeful in that it would obviously reflect a system established in the larger context of the class and its curriculum.

## Justifying Book Clubs

No one becomes an English teacher just to help students meet instructional standards and do well on high-stakes tests. Instead, we do so because we love to read and write, or because of an eighth-grade English teacher, or because we read *To Kill a Mockingbird* in tenth grade and have never been the same.

I can't imagine a life without reading. As I look around the room where I am writing, every flat surface holds some kind of book. A thin novel and a book of essays lean against the stereo. A boxed set of picture books on the back of the piano serves as a pedestal for a framed quotation from Shakespeare's *Twelfth Night*. A trio of Mary Oliver's books rests on the end table, and my daughter's bible and my son's latest chapter book are stacked on the stairway leading to their bedrooms. The history I just finished and the memoir I'm working on are lying on the coffee table, and research books and journals are stuffed behind its cabinet doors. It's really not as messy as it sounds. It's just that books are fixtures in my family's lives. I want them to be so in the lives of adolescent readers as well.

We became English teachers because the words we read and write matter to us, and we want them to matter just as much to our students. Yet as the demands of standards, curricula, and standardized tests press in, we have to wonder what makes book clubs worth the time. For one thing, book clubs acknowledge these constraints rather than ignore them, but they do so by putting adolescent readers' needs first. In the next chapter, I identify these needs and describe how book clubs are designed to meet them.

# 2

# The Moment at Hand

*Meeting Adolescent Readers Where They Are*

The Russian psychologist Lev Vygotsky (1978) is probably best known for his concept of the "zone of proximal development," that teachable space that lies between what students are able to accomplish by themselves and what they can accomplish with the help of a more capable other. Like many teachers these days, I've been strongly influenced by Vygotsky's ideas about learning because I've seen them played out repeatedly in those teaching moments I've deemed successful. I like to think of these as "moments in the zone," when I meet my students where they are. Prior moments also hover around, informing the present by reminding me of where the learners have been. Potential moments direct my teaching, too, by suggesting where learners might go next. If I focus too much on what's hovering in the past or future, however, I lose sight of all we really have—the moment at hand, for that moment contains the point of need, and the point of need is where teachers can make a difference.

If I'm honest, though, I have to admit external constraints also crowd the moment at hand. The standards movement, for instance, was conceived with the future in mind because standards delineate what students should know and be able to do. The accountability movement, on the other hand, focuses on the past by attempting to determine what students *do* know and *have* done, usually through one-shot attempts on high-stakes standardized tests. Both movements attempt to direct the present but with an eye toward what adult experts need from kids rather than the other way around.

Politicians have equated standards and accountability with educational reform so much that neither movement is going away anytime soon, regardless of how teachers might feel about their undue influence on what teachers have been thrust into a game not of their own choosing, but they need to know the game inside and out because they still have to play by the rules. But teachers must always, always remember that the ball they're keeping their eyes on is *learning*, not testing.

The challenge, then, lies in figuring out how to do our job and still be able to sleep at night. By that I mean that one of the most important questions we must answer on a daily basis is this: What teaching and learning practices will help my students grow as readers and writers and at the same time prepare them to demonstrate what they know and are able to do? In other words, we need to identify and create a classroom environment where we can implement authentic practices that will lead to student achievement.

But in this chapter, I'd like to focus not on the past or the future, but on the moment at hand. Let's face it: standards were written by adults for adults as goals and guidelines that should inform curriculum development, classroom instruction, and assessment. But in listing what kids should know and be able to do in order to demonstrate their literacy prowess, standards don't always spell out what adolescents need in the first place.

If we are to have a prayer of engaging readers so that they can meet standards, we should look at what research tells us about what adolescent readers need. I need to offer a disclaimer, though. No study, no book, and certainly no chapter can tell us once and for all how to meet all kids' needs for reading. But that doesn't mean we have to stand around wringing our hands, wondering what in the world we're actually supposed to *do* in our classrooms.

As I've written elsewhere (O'Donnell-Allen 2005), few and far between are those practices that will work in exactly the same manner in one classroom as they worked in another. The best we can do is articulate a cohesive set of principles based on theory and research that can serve as a framework for our teaching. That's what I try to do in this chapter. But it's always up to teachers to make use of theory and research in light of the contexts in which we teach and the students that inhabit them.

To get a full picture of adolescent readers' needs, I turn to the instructional framework described by Ruth Schoenbach, Cynthia Greenleaf, Christine Cziko, and Lori Hurwitz (1999) in *Reading for Understanding: A Guide to Improving Reading in Middle and High School Classrooms.* They identify four interactive dimensions of classroom life necessary for developing strategic adolescent readers—social, personal, cognitive, and knowledge-building dimensions—and describe metacognitive conversation as the glue that holds them together. Because these dimensions are so helpful in describing how we can meet adolescent readers' needs in the moment at hand, I use them in the following sections to organize a discussion around the following questions:

What do adolescent readers need to thrive and grow?

How can book clubs help them become more willing, engaged, and strategic readers?

## The Social Dimension of Reading

The social dimension of reading refers to the connections students make (or don't make) in the context where the act of reading occurs. This context includes the actual classroom environment and their relationships to the peers and adults within it. It's important to note, however, that our classrooms overlap with other contexts within the school, such as peer and cultural groups, clubs and organizations, and so on, and that they are also nested within larger social contexts outside of school, including local communities and race, class, and gender designations in the culture at large. In this book, however, I focus on what teachers can do to nurture the social aspects of students' reading development *within a classroom environment.* Consequently, I think it's important to start with the source, adolescents themselves.

### What Students Need and How Book Clubs Can Help

What kind of social environment do students say they need? A long-term survey of reluctant but capable adolescent readers identified the following characteristics of teachers and classrooms that motivated them to read (Lesesne and Buckman 2001, 106):

| | |
|---|---|
| Classroom libraries: | 75% |
| Time to read at school: | 80% |
| Listening to books on tape: | 55% |
| Teachers who read aloud daily: | 80% |
| Teachers who allow selection in reading material: | 90% |
| Teachers who ask me what I like to read: | 100% |

| | |
|---|---|
| Teachers who read the books I recommend: | 65% |
| Teachers who have us talk about books in class: | 45% |
| Teachers who are "caught" reading: | 55% |
| Places to curl up with books in class: | 55% |

I've grouped these classroom characteristics into three broader categories: (1) access to books and time to read them, (2) opportunities for self-expression and social interaction, and (3) physical comfort and emotional safety. Interestingly, students' responses to Lesesne and Buckman's survey mirror many of the research findings and the recommendations of professional organizations.

**ACCESS TO BOOKS AND TIME TO READ THEM** Position statements by the International Reading Association (Moore et al. 1999), National Council of Teachers of English (1999), and the National Middle Schools Association (IRA and NMSA 2002) unanimously recommend that adolescents be given access to a wide range of texts that reflect their abilities, interests, and cultural and linguistic diversity. Students with greater access to books tend to read more, students who read more tend to improve as readers, and reading improvement tends to spill over into other areas of literacy development, including writing (NCTE Commission on Reading, 2004b).

Without breaking the bank, book clubs can provide students access to a range of texts. For the same amount that a school would spend on a class set of *The Adventures of Huckleberry Finn* or some other title, teachers can select a small number of titles that are unified in some way (e.g., by theme, issue, author, or genre) yet still provide a range of reading opportunities in terms of style, cultural diversity, difficulty level, and content. Furthermore, by selecting from a range of books, students can pursue books according to their interests and abilities. Even though I've sometimes wondered if I should steer students away from books I suspect will be too difficult for them, I've found that the motivation to read a particular book, combined with the support students receive in book club, are often incentives to "read up." As long as students have had the chance to preview a book thoroughly so they know what they're getting into, I say that if they really want to read a book, they should get the chance to do so, even if it means that teachers may have to provide additional support, such as books on tape, if and when the going gets tough.

With jobs, extracurricular activities, practices and lessons, and multimedia competing for their attention outside of school, students also need time—in-school time—to read (Moore et al. 1999). As my students have taught me, book clubs and sustained silent reading (SSR) programs are natural complements. To be effective, SSR time must be provided on a regular basis, and students will need guidelines for how to spend it (McQuillan et al. 2001). Although most SSR programs recommend allowing students to choose texts carte blanche (and this isn't a bad idea for another day), the practice is easily adapted to give students time to read their book club books for ten to fifteen minutes per class period, usually at the start of class.

In Lesesne and Buckman's survey, students also expressed a preference for teachers who read aloud to them on a regular basis. Book clubs provide authentic contexts for this practice as well, though in this case, students rather than teachers are the ones reading aloud. I've never observed a book club where students didn't read passages spontaneously in service of a larger point or just for sheer enjoyment.

### OPPORTUNITIES FOR SELF-EXPRESSION AND SOCIAL INTERACTION

Penny Oldfather (1993) followed a group of students from fifth grade through high school in order to discover what kinds of classroom contexts motivated them to learn. She found that students were most motivated by classrooms that cultivated *honored voice*, in other words, that gave students opportunities to express themselves with the assumption that they had valuable things to say. By design, book clubs reinforce Oldfather's assumption of *honored voice*, equipping students with the strategies and authority to interpret texts and express what they think these texts mean. Students' need for self-expression is also reinforced by giving students choice in what they read, an aspect of book clubs I discuss in detail later in this chapter when describing students' personal needs as readers.

Opportunities for self-expression and social interaction go hand in hand. As anyone who has worked with adolescents knows, the majority of them are wired to connect. Without any prompting by adults, they pass notes, talk on their cell phones, email, and instant message, occasionally all at the same time. Megan Baker, an experienced junior high teacher I know, explains it this way: "Kids love to talk, mainly to one another. Teachers just have to figure out how to use that against them." As Megan figures it, students' drive to interact with one another is so strong, they will find ways to whisper and pass notes even when the classroom is set up so that all desks are facing the front, the better to hear the teacher. So why not structure our classrooms to capitalize on most adolescents' intense interest in their peers and their opinions?

The research concurs. Smith and Wilhelm (2002) point out that "[l]iteracies grow out of relationships—whether these are teacher to student, student to student, parent to child, or mentor to mentee" (199). Students need opportunities for social interaction around meaningful literacy tasks in supportive contexts, especially because such approaches to teaching literacy content have been linked to student achievement (Applebee et al. 2003).

Through self-expression and social interaction in book clubs, students learn to examine texts critically, make personal and intertextual connections, and realize that complex texts can be interpreted in diverse ways. Of course anyone who has used small groups in the classroom knows that adolescents (or *human beings* of any age for that matter) do not learn collaboratively by chance. In Chapter 5, I discuss strategies for helping students establish book club norms and work together productively.

**PHYSICAL COMFORT AND EMOTIONAL SAFETY** Imagine for a moment that you have the entire morning off simply to read for pleasure. Where are you sitting? How's your posture? What about the light? Are you eating or drinking? Do you prefer music or silence?

Me, I'm in one of two places—the reclining corner of the overstuffed living room couch or propped up on multiple pillows on my side of the queen-sized bed. The lighting is natural or incandescent, I have either a steaming cup of tea or an icy can of Diet Coke on the nearby table, and my snoring dog is curled up at my feet.

I'm guessing you didn't picture yourself folded into an unforgiving plastic chair with a student desk attached to it either, no food or drink nearby, and no sound except for the buzzing fluorescent lights above. Yet this is how we most often expect kids to read in school. If you provide students with some SSR time to read their book club books, however, they're likely to appreciate your consideration of their comfort.

Elementary teachers and bookstore owners long ago realized that bean bags or cushiony armchairs, end tables, soft background music, and well-stocked bookshelves go a long way toward creating spaces where readers want to linger. Even though we're supposed to get serious about students' literacy development in secondary schools, we'd do well to remember that more than half of the adolescents surveyed by Lesesne and Buckman (2001) said they'd be more willing to read in a classroom where they could "curl up with books."

Fortunately, you don't need a degree in interior design to create an inviting reading environment. Probably the best reading environment my students and I ever created in the several classrooms I occupied over the years was located in the cruddiest wing of the school. One year during a major school remodel, I shifted classrooms three times, moving from a comfortable carpeted room to one end of the still full-service library to an old business classroom with crumbling floor tiles, ancient typing tables, and wooden chairs older than I was. The first day they visited their "new" room, thirty sixteen-year-olds were shocked into complete silence.

So my students and I decided to roll up our sleeves and get to work. Over the course of a couple of weeks, we raised enough loose change to buy an imitation oriental rug from a street vendor and a couch, a chair, and an end table from the student council garage sale. Students donated a microwave, plants, and an aquarium, and we sponge-painted one cinder-block wall to resemble the sky. Some students still chose to sit at their desks during SSR, but others vied for the couch or the chair, and some preferred to stretch out on the rug or lean against the wall. As long as they were comfortable and reading (not sleeping or doing math homework), I allowed them to choose where they wanted to settle.

Of course, if your surroundings are more opulent than these, you probably have other options. The room I just described was reasonably large, but even in a smaller room, students can make themselves more comfortable if you simply allow them to read on the carpeted floor, for instance. Temporary redecorating is also an option. Last year, my daughter's junior high teacher took a do-it-yourself approach, giving students permission to bring in a small pillow, a snack, and a good book on SSR days.

Even more important than creating a physically comfortable environment, however, is nurturing one that is emotionally safe. While safe-haven classrooms typically associated with student-centered practices have been challenged as intellectually soft in recent years, some believe students, especially girls, would benefit from classrooms turned into what Mary Louise Pratt (1991) terms "contact zones" (Finders 1997). These contact zones are "social spaces where cultures meet, clash, and grapple with each other, often in contexts of highly asymmetrical relations of power" (Pratt 1991, 34). Although I agree that girls need classrooms where their available roles extend beyond keeping the peace, I worry that contact zones represent the other extreme and some girls (and boys) will retreat into silence if confrontation is the norm, just as many girls have for years (Belenky et al. 1986). Secondary schools are legally charged to keep their classrooms physically safe, and I believe that secondary teachers are ethically charged to keep their classrooms emotionally safe as well.

But does this mean kids shouldn't be allowed to disagree?

Heavens, no.

A happy medium exists between the haven made so safe it is no longer challenging and the combative-sounding contact zone. Students will need help with this, but book clubs can provide a context where critical discussion and negotiation can occur. To help students feel comfortable taking interpretive risks and sharing their struggles with the texts they read, teachers might ask for students' help in generating rules of respect in classroom discussion and insist on a zero-tolerance policy for adolescents' one-liner put-downs as well (Beers 2003).

As I've found by observing book club discussions in many secondary classrooms, students can and will challenge each other and sharpen their own points of view when they feel the freedom to construct their own literary interpretations. When teachers ask students to pay explicit attention to book club norming, we can help them create book clubs where conflict can be productive and safety includes the freedom to respectfully challenge and disagree with one another. Furthermore, book clubs can help students consider alternative readings of texts. Particularly when we teach strategies for viewing texts through the lenses of various critical theories, students are freed up from the role of status quo reader. By thinking about how texts attempt to position them as readers and understanding the consequences, adolescents can choose how they wish to position themselves.

Finally, watching other readers grapple with texts in book clubs helps students realize that our classrooms are places where they can feel free to talk, listen, and compose their way to understanding. Because teachers have so often read and reread the texts we teach in whole-class settings, students can easily get the impression that we arrived at our nuanced interpretations the first time we read the book. Consequently, they may feel reluctant to reveal their own half-baked interpretations the minute they walk in the door unless we create classrooms where the hard work of reading and interpretation is acknowledged and supported. Teachers can serve as reading role models in this regard by describing their reading preferences, admitting their own reading struggles, and making their problem-solving processes visible through think-alouds prior to book club sessions (IRA and NMSA 2002). Students also learn strategies indirectly from their peers because the bulk of conversation during book clubs tends to uncover how their classmates are making sense of texts. In Chapter 5, I share specific response tools that prompt exploratory talk, writing, and visualizing.

## The Personal Dimension of Reading

The personal dimension of reading refers to students' relationship to reading as individuals. What do they think of reading? How do they see themselves as readers? The primary aspects of this dimension are developing a reader's identity and self-awareness and providing for personal choice (Schoenbach et al. 1999).

### What Students Need and How Book Clubs Can Help

Helping students establish reader identities and develop self-awareness as readers is key to their motivation and development. To understand who they are as readers, students need to share their reading histories, preferences, and strengths and weaknesses for themselves and others. When the reading gets tough (and they need to know that the reading gets tough for everyone at some point in time), students must be able to connect their efforts to their own goals and interests. Otherwise, they are unlikely to persist in developing the confidence and stamina necessary to read a wide range of challenging texts (Schoenbach et al. 1999).

Reflective activities, such as reading inventories and goal setting, not only help students better understand themselves as readers but also provide teachers with invaluable information. When Jeff Wilhelm (1997) began routinely administering attitude inventories to his junior high students, he was astonished to find that approximately half preferred not to read on their own because of negative experiences in school where reading was reduced to finding the "right" answer. Even willing readers made distinctions between "school reading" and "real reading," identifying reading for pleasure as something they did only outside of school.

As helpful as this kind of information may be in figuring out how to meet the needs of our readers, we can get it only by asking for it. Reading inventories fit naturally into classrooms implementing a book club approach. While I've found Nancie Atwell's (1998) inventory to work well prior to book clubs, I've also invited parents to write letters at the start of the school year to help me better understand their children as readers, writers, and human beings.

Setting and monitoring goals for individual reading development and book club participation are also effective ways to enhance students' identities and self-awareness as readers. Goal-setting activities can help students identify authentic reasons for reading connected to their life goals (Schoenbach et al. 1999). Other activities, many of which simply involve making topics such as metacognition, fluency, stamina, confidence, and reading range fair game for classroom discussion, can help students gain better control over their reading processes and persistence when reading difficult texts. By bringing these topics into book clubs as well, we help students see that "all readers, including the teacher, are developing readers and that everyone has room to grow during a lifetime of reading" (29).

In every aspect of life, developing identity and self-awareness necessarily involves agency, the power to make one's own choices. Likewise, to know who you are as a reader, you must know the kinds of books you like to read. As my husband loves to remind our children (who are usually rolling their eyeballs at the time), the choices we make determine who we are. If we extend this principle to reading, do teachers or students ultimately get to determine who the students are as readers?

Like adults, students need to be interested in what they're studying, to understand why it is useful and relevant to their own lives, and to feel competent while they're doing it. This means they need opportunities to read what they choose at least part of the time. Reluctant adolescent readers agree. In fact, 90 percent of the reluctant readers surveyed by Lesesne and Buckman (2001) reported that having a say in what they read made a difference in their motivation to read.

While some might argue that students have plenty of time to choose their own books outside of school, a growing number of *people*, not just adolescents, choose not to read outside of school at all. The reasons reading is eschewed by *aliterate* students—those who can read but choose not to—include lack of time, inability to find the right book, negative attitudes toward reading, and reading difficulty. To entice aliterate students to read, teachers must provide time to read in class, connect books to students' interests, and stress the enjoyment and emotional benefits of reading (Beers 2003).

One of the obvious ways that book clubs promote student interest and enjoyment of reading is by giving them a choice in what they read in school, the only place they may be doing any reading at all. The choice need not be entirely open-ended, however. Rather, Lesesne and Buckman repeatedly heard kids saying, "let us have some limited selection" (2001, 107). In fact, struggling readers in particular can feel overwhelmed by an all-you-can-eat buffet of books. They need help from teachers in narrowing down their choices based on their interests. I discuss practical methods for managing these choices in Chapter 4.

## The Cognitive Dimension of Reading

The cognitive dimension of the reading process refers to the set of skills and strategies students use to make sense of texts and gain independent control of their reading processes (Schoenbach et al. 1999).

### What Students Need and How Book Clubs Can Help

To become or continue to be willing and able readers as they progress through the upper grades, adolescents need an extensive repertoire of skills and strategies that will help them negotiate the increasingly complex materials they will encounter in school and the world beyond (IRA and NMSA 2002). Before we consider how these skills and strategies ought to be taught in schools, let me ask you a question: In your daily paper, do you find multiple-choice questions you must answer to gauge your degree of reading comprehension?

I didn't think so. That's because your understanding of the paper's content is more likely to be measured by your ability to carry on a conversation about it with another family member over a bowl of oatmeal. Yet in traditional reading instruction, cognitive skills and strategies are often taught in isolation, apart from application to authentic texts (i.e., texts that weren't created only for instructional purposes). To illustrate, let me draw on my experiences with reading instruction as a student. In the seventies, when I grew up, cognitive research and individualized reading instruction were all the rage, so my middle school classmates and I got to learn to read out of a box. I was an avid reader outside of school, and the only part of my reading class that I could tolerate was the end of the period when my teacher apologetically departed from the curriculum to read aloud from her brother-in-law's books for children. Thank goodness her family pride trumped educational progress because by this time, I'd learned to hate Reading with a capital R—school reading, that is—as opposed to reading with a lowercase r, which was something I did on my own time.

I can't imagine two activities that had less in common. In school reading, I took a pretest that determined from which box I would grab booklets like *Reading in Context* and *Finding the Main Idea.* Every day I located a study carrel and focused on the booklet and its corresponding strategy du jour. As quickly as possible, I read brief passages written by voiceless authors and raced through the insipid quizzes that followed. Having finished Reading, I was finally able to return to my desk and *really* read in context my Nancy Drew mysteries or omnipresent Scholastic paperback, presumably grasping the main idea. There were no quizzes. And I was back in bibliophilic heaven.

Aside from my teacher's voice reading aloud, the defining characteristic of my middle school reading instruction was silence. Ostensibly, I was getting the best education that money could buy, since I was learning reading strategies tied to my individual level of reading. Yet I saw absolutely no connections among the reading aloud I tolerated, the workbooks I abhorred, and the personal reading I couldn't get enough of.

Though less common across the board these days, my experiences are still played out in remedial reading programs and study-skills classes required of all students in many secondary schools. I think this is because schools have heeded only part one of the research on reading: cognitive researchers have identified the components of skilled readers' processes, and these strategies can indeed be taught.

But wait, there's more! As my own experiences bear out, part two of these findings reveal what's most important: when taught in isolation, skills-based instruction has little impact on reading development and no discernible relationship to one's actual reading process (Schoenbach et al. 1999). Teachers need to "*un-teach* kids . . . the part-to-whole strategies they learned in the scope and sequence of their early reading classes. They need to discover ways to make reading literature in school more like reading at home" (Hynds 1997, 47). Literacy instruction is most effective in inquiry-oriented contexts in which students have immediate opportunities to apply skills and strategies toward authentic texts and meaningful ends (Smith and Wilhelm 2002).

An AP English teacher I know is fond of saying that the bigger the box of teaching materials that comes with the adopted literature anthology, the farther and faster teachers need to run. That's because these "ancillary" materials can quickly take the place of the actual text. Unfortunately, until schools create opportunities for kids to apply their repertoire of cognitive skills and strategies to real books, learning to read out of the box will continue. In the meantime, textbook companies, not kids, will reap the rewards.

The best way to help students make the connections between the strategies I "learned" in my study carrel and the reading I did at my desk is through the kind of *embedded instruction* a book club approach provides. Book clubs help students learn a variety of skills and strategies, not in a workbook or an isolated exercise, but *within the context of actual use*. The embedded nature of this instruction is key because students can know about strategies without knowing how to apply them. In fact, research shows that students need "systematic guided practice in strategy use *while they are engaged in answering their content area questions*" (Hynds 1997, 37). In the section on metacognitive conversation (page 33) and for the rest of this book, I talk more about how book clubs lend themselves naturally to this kind of guided practice.

## The Knowledge-Building Dimension of Reading

The knowledge-building dimension of the reading process refers to three types of knowledge readers need to fully comprehend a text (Schoenbach et al. 1999):

1. knowledge about the text's content (what the text says)

2. knowledge about the text's structures (how the text works)

3. knowledge of disciplinary habits of mind (how the text expects the reader to work)

### Knowledge About Content: What Students Need and How Book Clubs Can Help

When students are reading texts that are likely to contain unfamiliar content, teachers can provide relevant background information, but students can also conduct small-scale research on relevant topics prior to book club. For example, seventh-grade girls in one after-school book club researched various aspects of medieval culture and taught what they learned to one another before reading Cushman's 1994 novel *Catherine Called Birdy* (Beach and Myers 2001). Research can also be helpful during and after reading the book. Students in my adolescent literature course were largely unfamiliar with Iranian culture when they began reading *Persepolis*, Marjane Sartrapi's autobiography written in graphic form. While reading, they identified familiar topics that had been made somehow unfamiliar to them in the context of the book (e.g., religion, education, gender, media images, etc.). They then researched these topics and integrated their findings into cultural studies presentations to teach themselves, their classmates, and me more about the book and its cultural context, as well as our own.

Even when the content of a text is familiar, activating students' prior knowledge can help them become invested in a text before they read it. Before my high school seniors read *Hamlet*, I asked them to imagine the following scenario and freewrite for ten minutes about how they would feel and react if they were in similar circumstances:

> You've come home from college on spring break to discover that your mother has remarried, even though your father died only a few short months ago. She didn't marry just any old guy, though. She's chosen your uncle, and by the way the newlyweds are acting, you'd think your father never existed. To make matters worse, they don't understand why you're so depressed. They tell you to quit being such a Gloomy Gus and to think of your uncle as your father. They also ask a couple of kids you knew from high school to keep an eye on you in case you decide to do anything stupid. To top it all off, your own true love's father has forbidden you to see her or him, and your best friends from high school think you might be going crazy.

After students finished freewriting, we talked about what they had written. Students always got engaged in this discussion, sometimes making connections to parents' divorces and covering a gamut of emotions from grief to confusion, betrayal to anger. Inevitably, though, some student would say, "Man, I'd want to kill they guy!" That's when I'd respond, "Then you know exactly how Hamlet felt." Priming the emotional pump in this way helped students develop empathy not just for Hamlet but for other characters in the play as well. When Peter Smagorinsky and I studied transcripts of students' small-group discussions, one group of girls commiserated with Ophelia. They talked about her as if she were one of their teenage friends, referring to her as "that poor thing" whose boyfriend "dumped" her (O'Donnell-Allen and Smagorinsky 1999).

Although I take this example from a text read by the entire class, the strategy is easily adaptable to a book club context. In fact, prereading activities are ideal for the first book club meeting, when students have selected books but have not begun reading them yet. Writing to similar prompts tailored to their respective books and then discussing them with their book clubs is but one way to spark interest and emotional investment in characters' circumstances. Numerous other prereading activities, such as opinionnaires and case studies, can help prepare students for texts with familiar content (Smagorinsky, McCann, and Kern 1987).

## Knowledge About Text Structures: What Students Need and How Book Clubs Can Help

Even though *reading* and *writing* are almost always used as intransitive verbs in common parlance (e.g., "students should read and write"), we are always reading something, that is, a particular text written by an author who has made assumptions about the reader's identity and her or his capacity for entering the text successfully (Gee 1989). Consequently, when it comes to learning to read, we are always doing so in the ways sanctioned by a particular "discourse community" that uses specialized language and values certain "ways of being in the world" (Gee, quoted in Cushman et al. 2001, 526).

As I write this sentence, for instance, I am assuming that you belong to the community of English education. You teach secondary language arts or you aspire to do so or you work with secondary language arts teachers. I suspect that you are interested in improving your own practice or helping others do so because you are taking time out from your busy life to engage in professional reading. I'd guess that you are open to new ideas for supporting kids as readers, and you've picked up this book to find out how book clubs might help. I also would bet that you're in the habit of professional reading. You might subscribe to professional journals, attend conferences where articles and books on literacy are cited, and have probably read *books like this* before so you *know what to expect* from this one.

Books like this. Know what to expect. What exactly do I mean?

I mean that these prior experiences as a member of the community of English education have undoubtedly caused you to develop certain expectations about the *genre* of pedagogical literature. Just as you expect plays to contain dialogue and dramatis personae and contemporary poetry to contain unrhymed end lines, you expect pedagogical texts to contain certain features like an introductory chapter that previews the content of subsequent chapters, references to other theory and research throughout the book, and practical applications of this theory and research in the form of teaching strategies.

These text features and expectations also influence how you are actually reading the book at this very moment. In fact, I bet they kicked into play before you even purchased it or checked it out from the library. By habit, you probably read the back of the book and skimmed the table of contents to see if it was something you could use. You may have dipped into a couple of chapters to look for promising strategies or to see if the writing was accessible. You might even have checked out the bibliography to see whether you approved of the authors I was citing or looked in the appendices for book lists or other helpful resources.

Now that you've decided to take the plunge, you may not be reading the book straight through from start to finish. You may have skipped the acknowledgments, where I thank some really nice people, because your own really nice people have demands on your time. If you're experienced with book clubs, you're probably skimming chapter headings and thinking, "Got this, know how to do that," until you come to a strategy you've never tried before or the specific resource you need. That's when you stop and read.

All this means that my job as a writer is to fulfill our unspoken contract by meeting your expectations for the genre of pedagogical literature or at least having a good reason for breaking the rules if I choose to. I need to keep the acknowledgments short, choose informative titles for the chapter headings and print them in bold, and make the strategies evident. In fact, right now I'm thinking, "Enough of the examples already. They get the picture, so make your point."

Here it is: To enter texts successfully, our students need to be able to do more than simply decode them. They also need knowledge about text structures and the disciplinary habits of mind it takes to comprehend them. The degree of help they need from us depends upon their familiarity with the genre at hand, the author's adherence to its typical conventions, and what we're asking them to actually do with the text.

Because they've grown up on nursery rhymes and Shel Silverstein, for example, students reading a collection of free-verse poetry in a book club may try to read it the same singsong way and are likely to be puzzled when thoughts aren't complete in the space of one or two lines. A minilesson on enjambment—the deliberate running over of a thought from one poetic line to the next—would help here, especially if the teacher modeled aloud how to read to the punctuation rather than pausing at the end of each line.

Students also need help when authors change the rules of the game. For instance, because they've told and listened to stories all their lives, students probably have an inherent understanding of the structure of conventional narratives. They likewise expect the stories they read to be chronological. But when those conventions are disrupted even on a minor scale—say, if the author employs a flashback without warning—students may need for teachers to draw explicit attention to the technique. Prior to book clubs, you might ask students to draw parallels to the ways television shows and films indicate that an event has happened in the past and to think about the purposes for doing so. Students could then compare these techniques and purposes with the author's use of flashback in their book club text. Another approach would be to ask book clubs to create a chronological time line of events in their text and then to compare this time line with the way these events are actually presented in the story. Asking book clubs to report out to the rest of the class after their discussion would allow students to see the multiple ways authors organize texts and to reflect on writerly purposes for, and readerly effects of, these stylistic choices.

### Knowledge About Disciplinary Habits of Mind: What Students Need and How Book Clubs Can Help

Finally, we need to make explicit for students that different communities and fields of study value different ways of thinking and behaving, and these in turn dictate the methods a reader must use to comprehend the texts these communities and fields produce. In order to understand a scholarly article on stem cell research, for instance, one must learn to read like a scientist. In order to interpret a sonata, one must read like a musician, and so on.

Although I agree that students should read a wide range of texts, for the purposes of this book, I'm assuming that students are reading literary texts in book clubs. Once we've moved beyond basic comprehension, then, we are charged with apprenticing students to the field of literary study. So we must pose these questions: How do literary scholars think? What language and methods do they use to appreciate, analyze, critique, and evaluate texts? How do they share their findings and interpretations with their colleagues?

The best way to apprentice students to new discourse communities is through a balance of formal teaching and enculturation (Gee 1989). In other words, memorizing literary terms and underlining similes in isolated passages is not enough if we want to invite students into the field of literary study. They also need to examine full-length texts in the company of other readers. Minilessons like those I described earlier, followed by immediate application of the concepts in book clubs, are one way to apprentice students to our discipline. I describe several other strategies in the chapters to come. My point here, though, is that because book clubs provide multiple opportunities for embedded instruction, they can obviously help.

## Reading and Metacognitive Conversation

Admittedly, getting adolescent readers to read and respond can seem like enough of a task without asking them to reflect on the process as well, but metacognitive conversation—"talking together about making sense of texts"—allows students "to become aware of their reading processes and, indeed, that there are reading processes" (Schoenbach et al. 1999, 23).

### What Students Need and How Book Clubs Can Help

Although adolescents intuitively use a variety of skills and strategies when they read even simple texts, they may not realize they are doing so. Students can become better, more confident readers, however, if they are able to

- develop awareness of the reading strategies at their disposal

- know how and when to use these strategies

- evaluate the effectiveness of a selected strategy for particular texts and contexts

- adapt the strategy accordingly

Students also need to understand that reading, composing, talking, and listening are interrelated processes. Metacognitive conversation can help students raise awareness of their reading processes, strategy use, and the interrelated nature of literacy behaviors (Hynd 1999).

Teachers can use classroom discussions as well as written conversations with texts and other readers to make students' thinking explicit for themselves and one another (Schoenbach et al. 1999). By building metacognitive conversation into book clubs, teachers help students become gradually more independent in their use of reading strategies. This process can be as simple as modeling the use of a given strategy and then asking students to practice it in small groups before they try it by themselves.

For instance, when introducing my high school students to double-entry reading logs, I first modeled writing a log entry on an overhead transparency in front of the class. I talked about when and where I might use the strategy and then read a brief poem or passage from a familiar text and thought aloud about which part I should select for my journal entry. I demonstrated how to record enough of the passage on the left side of the page so that I'd have a sense of it later, how to use an ellipsis to indicate the phrases I was omitting, and how to record the page number so I'd be able to find the passage again when necessary. Then, I reacted to the passage by talking about why I found it to be important, confusing, or otherwise striking. Because I wanted students to understand the provisional, exploratory nature of this process, my response intentionally wasn't streamlined. Instead I let them hear the inevitable stops, starts, questions, and revisions even experienced readers make as they work toward interpretations. I modeled asking questions and working toward provisional interpretations on paper as I recorded on the right side of the page my reactions to the quotation I'd selected earlier.

Next, I asked students to get into small groups and go through the same process, creating a reading log on a transparency in response to another brief passage or poem. While students were working, I browsed the room, eavesdropping and answering questions. Next, groups shared their work on the overhead, and the other students and I commented on what we found helpful, insightful, or problematic in their responses. If this was students' first experience with reading logs, I often had to troubleshoot by pointing out where they had simply paraphrased rather than interpreted, and we talked about various strategies for rectifying this problem. Students then completed individual reading logs for the next section of their book and brought them the next day as stimuli for class discussion.

The same approach works well when introducing students to new response tools prior to a book club cycle. After students try out the tool for the first time and discuss their responses in book club, I ask them to reflect on how these individual responses influenced the discussion. Students circle passages from their individual responses that actually were discussed by their group. Then, in whole-class discussion, we consider questions such as these:

- Which topics generated extended discussion and which ones fizzled out?

- In both cases, what made the difference?

- How might these reactions guide your individual responses to the next passage of your book club book?

This example illustrates how book clubs naturally lend themselves to multiple layers of metacognitive conversation, serving as a scaffold to move students from teacher support to independent application of reading strategies. First, students *develop awareness* of a new strategy they can use. Second, through the teacher think-aloud, students *gain information about how and when to use the strategy* and an inside look into the mind of an experienced reader implementing it. They benefit from whole-class feedback as they try the strategy out for the first time in the safety of a small-group setting before they are asked to try it alone. Then, they *evaluate the effectiveness* of their first attempts after seeing how their journal played before a live audience in the actual book club. Finally, based on these individual reflections and feedback from the whole-class discussion that follows, students are able to *identify what adjustments they need to make* in subsequent responses. Throughout the process the interrelationships among reading, writing, talking, and listening are made abundantly clear.

## Coming Back to the Moment at Hand

The research cited previously makes clear that book clubs are a theoretically sound approach to teaching literature. By addressing adolescents' social, personal, cognitive, and knowledge-building needs in a meaningful context at the point of use, book clubs can help students develop into more willing, engaged, and strategic readers. As students in book clubs move beyond their individual responses to consider those of their peers who have chosen to read the same book, they are likely to arrive at new interpretive planes they couldn't have reached alone. But regardless of how well book clubs should work in theory, if they are to make an actual difference in an adolescent reader's development, what matters is how they play out in practice. In the next chapter, I recount the evolution of book clubs in my multiple classrooms over the years, beginning with my early experiments with my high school students and continuing all the way up to my present-day book clubs.

# 3

# Looking Back

## A Book Club Travelogue

When I began teaching, I had the mindset of many of my current college students who are studying to become teachers. I wanted to find out what worked in the classroom, and I wanted to go out and do it. I wanted to emerge as victorious as Robin Williams in *Dead Poet's Society* or Michelle Pfeiffer in *Dangerous Minds* (both English teachers, interestingly enough) by being *the* teacher who made *the* difference in my students' literate lives. In the movie of my teaching that played inside my head, I saw myself standing in front of a black, oak-framed chalkboard inside my high-ceilinged classroom. My brow was furrowed, my voice passionate. I mean I was *really teaching* as my students looked raptly on. The soundtrack was appropriately moving, something triumphant with strings.

Twenty years later, cue needle scratching record.

I must say I no longer really believe that bona fide *best* practices exist, even in the case of book clubs. *Consistently reliable* is a more accurate description of instructional approaches I use on a regular basis, such as writing workshops, multigenre research papers, and portfolios. Classroom life is just too unpredictable to come with any guarantees. My college students find this terribly unsettling. But I'm still in the classroom because I believe in "practice in process" (Fecho 2004, 6). Every class, every day, every year is different, which means I never get bored and I never have to stop learning. I haven't lost my faith in the belief that I (and the profession) can get better. One of the ways I do this is by learning from others' accounts of their teaching, especially the detailed ones that don't gloss over the complications, because they help me judge what degree of "pedagogical recycling" is necessary before trying a similar approach with my students in my classroom (O'Donnell-Allen 2005). Another way is through teacher research, that is, by systematically and intentionally inquiring into how I teach and how my students learn (Cochran-Smith and Lytle 1993).

Consequently, I've drawn on a hefty pile of data I've accumulated over the past fifteen years to reconstruct the detailed account of my book club experiences that follows—lesson plans, teaching journals, research questions, numerous drafts of response tools and assessments, student writing samples, and so forth. I offer this travelogue not to be self-indulgent or to imply that since I've got book clubs all figured out, all you need to do is get out there and replicate my journey. Rather, I hope that you will learn as much from the consistently reliable practice of book clubs as I have by juxtaposing my teaching circumstances, questions, beliefs, and practices with your own. Toward this end, I organize the following stages of my book club journey by the research questions that guided them.

## Do My Students See Themselves as Readers?

I was using book clubs in my high school classroom before I knew they had a name. Then as now, I hoped to inspire my students to become *readers for life* by providing them with in-school experiences that approximated those of readers outside of school. I didn't call them *book clubs* at the start, but I began using the approach in a rudimentary form in 1991, a few months after I read an article by Sydell Rabin (1990) in *English Journal*. Rabin didn't call them book clubs either. Rather, she described how she organized her students into "literature study groups" so they could agree upon a book to read and discuss together. Later that year, my mind returned to this appealing idea when I was faced with the departmental requirement of teaching a novel and the reality of several classes of students squirming toward the advanced stages of senioritis.

I decided to try what Donald Schön (1987) has referred to as a *frame experiment*. Just as the name suggests, these experiments allow teachers to frame messy instructional problems so that they can investigate certain aspects of the problems more closely, reflect on what they learn, and adjust their teaching accordingly. Frame experiments involve the following steps:

1. diagnosing students' current level of performance by asking the question, "Where are they in this area?"

2. setting some informed goals as a result by asking, "Where would I like them to be next?"

3. hypothesizing a set of strategies that might take students to this next level by considering "How can I get them there?"

4. making and implementing a plan based on this hypothesis by asking, "What's the best way to proceed?"

5. assessing the results of the sequence by examining the data collected along the way and reflecting on the question "How did it go?"

6. deciding what to do next by determining "What about my teaching should change or remain the same as a result?" (adapted from Hillocks 1995)

I should be clear here. In 1991, I was certainly familiar with the concept and necessity of reflection in my teaching. But just as I didn't refer to Rabin's (1990) literature study groups as book clubs from the start, I didn't refer to my book club experiment using Schön's terminology. Yet the inquiry-driven nature of this effort, the notes I made in my lesson plan book, and the data I collected in my "Novel Workshop" folder that year and the years that followed show that this was indeed a frame experiment.

Frame experiments may be "the basis of inquiry in teaching" (Hillocks 1995, 32), and I certainly had some questions about my senior students as readers at this point in the year at Norman High School, a large suburban school not far from the University of Oklahoma. Student demographics were what you might expect in a southwestern university town—mostly white, middle-class, native English speakers, with smaller percentages of African American, Latino, and Native American students. Although the makeup of honors classes was overwhelmingly white, my regular-track English classes typically reflected the demographics of the larger school, and my students were held in far less sway of the university's academic influence than its proximity might suggest. By April of their senior year, students had been accepted to the colleges and universities they would attend the following year. For their few remaining weeks of high school, even the most dedicated among them were ready to take the academic path of least resistance. Because reading a novel wasn't the uppermost task in their minds, suffice it to say I had a challenge on my hands.

Still, this district requirement and my own pressing questions made me willing to try a new approach, even this late in the year. I had been using writing workshops in my classes, and I felt confident that, near the end of the year, my students saw themselves as writers and our class as a writing community. But, I wondered, did they feel the same way about reading?

I chose the literature that my students read in class although they had considerable freedom in how they responded to it, and I typically directed the whole-class discussions that followed. Sure, I had read Nancie Atwell's *In the Middle* (1998), but I had been unwilling to give up the lively interchanges I regularly witnessed in our class discussions for the seemingly more private practices of journal exchanges and individualized conferences that Atwell recommended for the reading workshop. Rabin's ideas in her *English Journal* article, however, seemed to offer hope for a happy compromise.

With the issue of ownership weighing heavy on my mind, I wanted my students to have the experience of reading independently and discussing their responses in small groups. I liked Rabin's strategies for incorporating student choice with curricular requirements by allowing students to choose their texts from a short list of those required by her district. I could also imagine how the independent response strategies my students were already using could easily dovetail with the process of collaborative interpretation. My fondest hope, however, was that my students would begin to *voluntarily* refer to themselves as readers and to see our class as a reading community. I wondered if it would be possible to adapt Rabin's literature study groups so that they would build on the momentum we had achieved in writing workshop. This question and Rabin's set of suggested strategies framed the experiment to follow.

Thinking my students might balk at any approach that included the word *study* this late in the spring of their senior year, I rechristened Rabin's literature study groups as the "novel workshop," adapted her basic approach for my students, and decided to give it a try. On the first day of the workshop, I presented book talks on titles I found in the English department book room and asked students to individually list their top three choices from among these titles. Based on their choices, I organized students into small groups. Students met with me in these groups twice a week and read independently on the other days. To prepare for their small groups, they created discussion questions, responded to short open-ended prompts I provided for each book, and completed double-entry reading logs as they had earlier in the year. At the end of the unit, students mined the reading log and wrote a formal literary analysis, also a district curriculum requirement, on a topic of their choice.

Notations from my lesson plans that year and the changes I made to these teaching materials in ensuing years show that this first frame experiment was a limited success. In regard to my original question about whether or not the novel workshop might build on the momentum we had achieved through writing workshop, I had glimpsed hints that the approach might provide the same elements of time, ownership, and community to readers that writing workshop had provided to writers in my classroom over the past few years. For one thing, some students had clearly begun to value in-class reading time as much as they valued in-class writing time during writing workshop. For another, students seemed to appreciate having a modicum of choice among books, even though most weren't terrible fired up about reading *On the Beach* or *Lord of the Flies*. Also, some students who seldom, if ever, spoke in whole-class discussion appeared more willing to share their ideas in the small group, and I could see that the rest of us had been missing out on their voices.

Still, there were problems. For one thing, my insistence on meeting with each small group was a scheduling nightmare. Let's just say it involved a matrix. Preparation was also a problem, as the homework I assigned for myself in my lesson plan book shows that I spent lots of late nights reviewing and responding to multiple novels while each of my students was reading only one. Furthermore, as I had pictured novel workshop in my head, my presence in the small group had seemed as necessary as it was in conferences during writing workshop. Yet, in practice, my presence in a small group resulted in my *absence* from the rest of my "angelic" students, who were supposed to be quietly reading on the other side of the room. I hadn't fully anticipated the classroom management problems that would result. Like a family chauffeur, I soon discovered how difficult it was to keep my eyes on the road of a small-group discussion and keep peace among a car full of restless adolescent readers at the same time. I also discovered that my presence seemed to inhibit rather than foster discussion. Even though I had been mindful about hanging back, students still looked quite literally at me rather than their classmates during our discussions, and the tentative nature of their voices suggested they were still seeking my approval for their interpretations. Even declarative statements, for instance, were phrased as questions: "Piggy and Ralph tried to use the conch shell to keep order?"

In the end, though, enough had gone right to convince me to make some adjustments and give novel workshops another try, and the questions that continued to emerge in the process persuaded me to recycle the frame experiment again and again in the years that followed. At this point, though, I wondered how having a real choice of texts rather than just a choice among the book room offerings might influence students' sense of themselves as readers and of our class as a reading community. Would their motivation to read increase if more contemporary titles were added to the mix?

# What Difference Does Choice Make?

The next year I presented my students with the idea of reading any book they wanted, within reason, the only condition being that any resultant purchases would have to come out of their pockets. Overwhelmingly, students chose to read "real books," as they referred to contemporary titles. I cajoled the assistant principal into covering costs if students couldn't afford this expense and persuaded the local bookstore to kick in a generous discount. I instructed students to shop around over the next week and come back with title recommendations by Friday, when they would lobby for their choices.

The first indication that real choices created real readers came much sooner than I had expected. I'll never forget that Friday when for the first time ever in my career, I heard students, even and especially the self-proclaimed nonreaders, arguing heatedly over which book they would *get* to read. Their final choices that year included *Forrest Gump*, *Congo*, and *The Client*. Students agreed on a reading schedule and wrote what I called Real Books Letters to record their personal responses in the form of a friendly letter written to a peer or me. In class, they alternated between sustained silent reading time and regular small-group discussions. Finally, they created Life Map murals—a modified version of an autobiographical prewriting exercise we'd completed earlier in the year (Kirby and Liner 1988)—to record the book's most significant events along the way (see Figures 3.1 and 3.2).

I reasoned that if I allowed students choices about what they were to read, I also ought to allow them choices in how to represent the meanings they had constructed throughout the novel workshop, so I decided not to restrict their final activity to the literary analysis paper as I had before. I had become intrigued by Howard Gardner's (1983) multiple intelligences theory and decided to take a risk. I provided an overview of the seven categories of intelligence Gardner had identified at the time and gave students free rein to construct a final project that drew on their intelligences and encapsulated their interpretations of the text they had read.

Hoping that students would maintain the enthusiasm I had seen from them up to this point in the workshop, I challenged them to think outside the box by asking themselves the following questions:

⊛ When you really want to get your point across, how do you best express it?

⊛ How do you best communicate outside of this class or outside of school altogether?

FIG. 3.1 *Forrest Gump Life Map*

FIG. 3.2 *Client Life Map*

⊛ When, where, and how do you feel most confident in showing what you know?

I suggested that their answers to these questions were likely to indicate where the most prominent of their multiple intelligences might lie. Even as I posed the questions, however, I was especially wary that students would respond to Gardner's theories simply to get themselves off the hook, reasoning something to the effect of "Well, I'm not good at writing analytical papers because I'm so good at playing basketball. Obviously, I only possess kinesthetic intelligence."

Consequently, I warned students about misusing Gardner's work and explained that the presence of one intelligence didn't necessarily indicate the absence of another. Rather, I suggested that it's helpful to think of one's intelligences in terms of potential. Just as a diamond in the rough holds promise, an individual has potential to develop multiple forms of intelligence. Shaped by cultural resources and experiences, personal predilections and abilities, certain facets of one's intelligence eventually emerge as more prominent than others. Even though some facets, or intelligences, are more visible, however, doesn't necessarily mean that others are nonexistent. One might simply need more time, effort, and support to bring the less visible facets to light. The most likely scenario, then, is that each of us possesses a *range* of intelligences, though in decidedly different degrees. In other words, this theory doesn't give a person the license to stop analyzing literature just because he or she is a gifted athlete, musician, or anything else for that matter.

For the purpose of the novel workshop, though, I wanted students to rely on their strengths, bringing their most prominent intelligences to bear on their culminating projects. I allowed students to work independently or collaboratively (as their intrapersonal and interpersonal intelligences dictated, of course) and provided a few class days for them to work on their projects with assistance. During presentation week, students shared these projects with the class and walked us through the Life Maps their small groups had created for their respective novels.

Predictably, very few students chose to write analytical papers. Instead, most created multimedia projects, ranging from a homemade video capturing crucial scenes from *The Client* to a scrapbook of Forrest Gump's life, complete with a dog tag and letters from Mama, to a trunk containing objects symbolic of crucial moments in *Congo*. Some of these projects gave evidence of hours of intellectual investment and plain old hard work. Others, like the pan of homemade lasagna meant to reflect attorney Reggie's Italian heritage in *The Client*, showed little evidence of interpretive grappling with the text. Still, superficial responses were the exception rather than the rule, and overall, I received some provisional answers to the original questions framing this experiment: Students *had* begun to show a real sense of community and reading motivation as they selected, read, and responded to their real books. Several even admitted to me that this was the first time in high school they'd finished a book, assigned or otherwise.

Again, I was mostly pleased with these results, especially the last one, but I wasn't exactly sure how to sustain this enthusiasm for the novel workshop, theirs or mine. I was still having difficulty keeping up with the reading, much less responding adequately to students' responses. Furthermore, I hadn't arrived at a satisfactory system that would allow me to keep track of multiple groups reading multiple novels. Based on the misgivings I'd previously felt about inhibiting student participation, I had replaced meeting with every group for an entire session to dropping in on them briefly but regularly on their discussion days. But I still couldn't visit every group and simultaneously maintain peace among the silent readers on the other side of the classroom, even with the help of a student teacher.

If I couldn't be everywhere at once, how could I be sure that students were engaged in substantive discussions? And what about the quality issue? Sure, students were eating up these books like candy and responding enthusiastically with multimedia projects, but were they becoming better readers as a result? This question led me to an even deeper worry: Which was more important, getting kids to read and respond, period, or getting them to read and respond critically? Although I knew I was on to something with novel workshops, I still wasn't sure how to satisfactorily reconcile these goals. Clearly, another frame experiment was on the horizon, but this one would have to wait a while as real life intervened in the form of my third child's birth and the completion of my master's degree.

## Can Real Readers Go It Alone?

I continued teaching the following year, but with a new baby in the house, I didn't have the time or energy to make many changes to the novel workshop. In the meantime, however, my colleague Gayle St. John and I attended a session at an Advanced Placement (AP) conference at which a presenter discussed independent student reading and analysis of multicultural books. Gayle and I were so excited by the seemingly rare prospect of choice in an AP classroom that Gayle wrote a grant to purchase several book sets to use in a similar fashion. Our AP senior English students teamed up in small groups to select a text that they would read and analyze together outside of class and afterward present in seminar format to their peers. We provided some general presentation guidelines, but the students' remarkably creative seminars demonstrated to us how capable they were of detailed, thoughtful, and independent analysis.

Although our AP students had substantial freedom in determining the content and format of their seminars, we had cued them to describe how identified themes played out within the novels. Perhaps because Gayle had intentionally selected multicultural titles, such as *A Yellow Raft on Blue Water*, *Their Eyes Were Watching God*, and *Things Fall Apart*, students noted thematic overlaps among these novels during the seminars, particularly in the areas of culture and identity. These overlaps proved especially useful for helping students make connections between their text and the ones they hadn't read since they were required to choose one of the other groups' novels for independent reading the following semester. This observation seemed incidental at the time, but it turned out to be instructive for my frame experiment on novel workshops the following year.

Through these seminars with my AP students, I gained some insight into my questions about novel workshop as well, even though I continued running the workshop as usual in my regular-track senior English classes that year. At least in my AP classes, adolescent readers appeared capable of going it alone in both discussion and analysis of complex literature. Their presentations had proved that. Then again, the students who chose to enroll in AP English were self-motivated almost by definition. How might the outcome of the literature seminars with my AP classes and the novel workshops with my regular-track English classes inform one another?

I wouldn't find out until the following school year when I shifted to junior English—both regular and AP classes—and began pursuing a doctoral degree in English education. These changes energized me again professionally, especially since I had founded a teacher-research group about the same time and had begun exploring professional texts on teacher research, such as *Inside/Outside* by Marilyn Cochran-Smith and Susan Lytle (1993), and *Changing Schools from Within*, by Gordon Wells (1994). As a result, my lingering questions regarding the novel workshop returned to the forefront of my mind, and I decided to implement the approach and another frame experiment with my junior AP class that spring.

The slight changes I made to the questions generated by my last frame experiment regarding textual complexity and critical response reflected the changes in my student population. The district book list for the honors track in junior English clearly implied that only complex works of literature were to be taught. Suffice it to say that *The Client, Congo*, and *Forrest Gump* were nowhere on the list. How, then, could I manage to include what I had begun to see as the indispensable element of choice? My AP senior English students had approached the independent reading and analysis of difficult texts with maturity in the literature seminar. But could I trust younger students to do the same during novel workshop discussions, and if they did, how could I keep track of what they said? Finally, what culminating assessments might allow them to draw on their multiple intelligences as my regular-track seniors had, while at the same time developing the advanced skills in literary analysis that an AP course required?

As I pondered these questions while preparing for novel workshop, I again reflected on the success of the literature seminars with my senior AP students. Finally, my brain clicked into gear. Part of the success of those seminars had stemmed from the thematic overlap among the novels. I had come to know my junior honors students as readers quite well by this point in the year. If I selected a short list of thematically related, complex novels that were likely to be appealing to them, perhaps I could ensure the requisite literary quality *and* preserve the element of choice, especially if the novels came from a range of time periods.

So this time, instead of allowing students to argue for any title under the sun, I chose a purposeful mix of titles organized around the theme of rebels, trailblazers, and scapegoats. After my brief book talks, students were allowed to thumb through and identify their top three choices from among *The Color Purple, One Flew over the Cuckoo's Nest, The Scarlet Letter*, and *A Yellow Raft on Blue Water*. I chose these texts not only because they reflected the unit theme but also because they were complex tales told well, just the sort of books that ought to raise important questions that these students would enjoy puzzling over together.

I also chose these titles because they contrasted in ways I knew would be appealing to this particular class. Most likely Chris, Billy, and the rest of their gang would be taken in by the battle between McMurphy and Big Nurse in *One Flew over the Cuckoo's Nest*. They were likely to find Chief's stream-of-consciousness narrative intriguing, especially when they heard that Ken Kesey had been a contemporary of Kerouac's (they'd been bugging me to teach the Beat poets all year long). On the other hand, Eliza, Maya, and others would almost certainly fall in love with Celie and connect with her fight for survival in *The Color Purple*, while students like Valerie and Nicki would be so troubled by the language, drug use, and explicit sexual content in that text that they would lose sight of its beauty. My guess was that these students would prefer the relative safety of *The Scarlet Letter*, especially because it had the added bonus of earning them another notch on their classic literature belts. Fortunately, others like Abe and Rachel wouldn't be daunted by the sheer heft of *A Yellow Raft on Blue Water*. Rather, they would wallow in Dorris' glorious language, then stand patiently by as he braided the disparate narratives into one.

As I used students' top three choices to determine their groups, I was relieved to discover that my predictions had been well founded. Students seemed enthusiastic rather than restricted by the titles. All that remained was to put the right mechanisms in place so that I could optimally manage the classroom while students analyzed the novels independently, discussed them in substantive ways, and shared their findings with their peers.

All that remained indeed. Fortunately, our school had moved to the block schedule by then—this teacher's dream come true since I could break each ninety-minute class into smaller, less hurried segments of time directed toward independent, small-group, or whole-class work as the task demanded. Consequently, I solved my perennial classroom management issues by allowing students twenty minutes at the beginning of class for SSR, finishing their Real Books Letters, or preparing individually for the forty-minute novel workshops that followed. We could then use the last thirty minutes for whole-class discussion or other tasks like vocabulary lessons. How should I organize the novel workshops, though?

Furthermore, what culminating assessment would best allow students to synthesize their collaborative interpretations and creatively present these to their peers? I recalled both the impressive multimedia projects my regular-track seniors had created and the insightful seminars generated by my AP senior English classes. As a result, I decided to ask my AP juniors to combine creative and analytical components in their final project. I asked them to do a readers' theatre script for one or more pivotal scenes from their text and to follow their performance with a panel discussion that critically analyzed these scenes and other significant issues or features present in the novel.

I was completely enamored with teacher research by this time, so I designed my questions regarding small-group discussion and culminating assessments in a more deliberate and systematic manner (Cochran-Smith and Lytle 1993). And this time, I decided to let my students in on my inquiry. I explained that I wanted to see what would happen when I allowed them to go it alone in their small-group discussions and that

I would be collecting data to see how it went. I planned to record my observations as field notes as I circulated the room, listening in on their discussions about their books. I would also collect their individual responses and discussion notes. Because the students expressed an interest in what I might find, I promised to share the results that emerged along the way.

It was at this point, then, that I mindfully took the simple frame experiment to the next level by conducting an informal teacher-research study in my classroom. As a budding qualitative researcher, I was comfortable with the term *data*, but this was the first time I'd ever referred to materials like student work, classroom artifacts, and the observations I routinely recorded in my lesson plans in such a way. Along with the fellow members of my teacher-research group, I was amazed at the degree of inquiry and agency this simple, but deliberate turn of phrase—and mind—lent to my teaching. As a teacher, not only could I pose my own questions, but, with the help of my students, I could also discover the answers and make changes that were likely to inform, and maybe even improve, the quality of learning in my classroom.

So as the novel workshop began, I took a vow of silence during students' small-group discussions as promised, stopping only to eavesdrop and make notations in my field notes. Even though I wasn't participating in students' discussions, I still couldn't be everywhere at once, so I devised the Novel Workshop Discussion Record to keep track of students' individual contributions to each discussion throughout the workshop. As well as providing additional data, this form allowed me to ask a common question across groups, one that would push students toward in-depth analysis and encourage them to see thematic connections among the novels later during their presentations. Finally, it provided a measure of accountability by signaling that I meant for students to stay on task.

Keeping my mouth shut proved much harder than I thought it would, but when I did, my researcher eyes and ears allowed me to see and hear what my teacher eyes and ears had failed to notice. Almost immediately, I made lasting changes in my instructional materials, namely in the form of the discussion record. I had initially listed questions like the one that follows at the top of the form, just above the space allotted for students' individual contributions:

First impressions are often lasting ones, especially when they are created by a storyteller whose voice is distinct. Consider the narrator's voice in the first section of your novel. From whose perspective is your story told? What makes the narrator's voice distinct? Why do you think the author chose this voice to tell her/his story, and what effects does this choice have on you as a reader?

Unfortunately, during the first small-group discussion, I observed that beginning with my question actually stunted rather than encouraged students' conversation. Discussion time had barely begun, and my field notes reveal this observation: "It's only 9:05, and no one is talking about *Yellow Raft*. They're obviously finished. Abe and Helena are studying for another class. Randy just put his handout away and is now listening to Rachel's stories. 'We're finished,' Rachel announced when I arrived, and now Helena wants to talk about painting. Can they handle this? Do we need to start smaller?"

Panic built; I moved on to the *Scarlet Letter* group, who were at least still attempting to discuss their novel. As the format of the discussion record directed, they began with my question, but the discussion was obviously stilted. Alicia identified the point of view as third person but sympathetic toward Hester. Silence. Marie bravely admitted that she didn't much care for the novel so far. More and longer silence. Finally, Valerie spoke up and observed that Hester is a rebel "because she stands up for herself and stays." Nicki immediately chimed in that Hester tries to be a trailblazer even though no one follows her. A promising start perhaps? But no. Just more and more silence. In my field notes, I remarked, "They seemed really stumped by my question. What if they started with their own responses instead? Maybe I need to change the form [of the discussion record]?"

Later, as I reread my field notes, I realized that most groups had gotten off to a rocky start in their first session. Such a clear pattern in their interaction—or I should more accurately say, in their *lack* of interaction—confirmed the questions I had asked while observing the *Scarlet Letter* group. I suspected that listing my question first had somehow prompted students to fish for the interpretive direction the question implied and, in the process, had shut down their own interpretations. So I decided to share this hunch with my students.

When I did, conversation opened up in ways I couldn't have anticipated. Yes, they admitted, it had been hard to start with a teacher question, especially when they hadn't anticipated the topic in their Real Books Letters, which then seemed inadequate as a result. Listing my question first made it seem like the most important, and if I really wanted to let them go it alone, I should change the format of the discussion record. They *weren't* ready to give up. They *did* believe they could handle steering their own discussions, and I was once again reminded of the mantra I'd repeatedly recorded in my teaching journal and the margins of my lesson plans during my first few years of teaching: "Trust your students, trust yourself."

When I did, the students did not disappoint. In analyzing their comments on subsequent discussion records, I discovered that they were making connections between their text and the unit theme, other texts they'd read, and their own lives. They had noted significant events and identified gender issues. They had traced key characters' development and shown extraordinary empathy for them in the process. They had even noted how the author's stylistic choices, such as Alice Walker's use of dialect in *The Color Purple*, influenced them as readers. Some of these observations were clearly in response to the questions I was providing at the bottom of the discussion record, but others they had come to completely on their own. Keeping my mouth shut appeared to be working.

My vow of silence was put to the test, however, as I eavesdropped on another book club discussion of *A Yellow Raft on Blue Water*. The students were discussing the effects of alcohol abuse on reservation life when Rachel, a generally sensitive and insightful white student, remarked that she wasn't surprised by this detail since it was "common knowledge that Indians can't hold their liquor." The prolonged silence that followed proved that I was not the only listener stunned by the blatant stereotype inherent in her claim.

I fidgeted in the chair I'd pulled up on the fringe of their circle and pressed my teacher lips shut in an effort to maintain my researcher vow of silence. "Give them a chance, and see what they will do," I reminded myself. And just about the time I was ready to cave in, Abe, God bless him, began in a gentle but insistent tone, "Rachel, I can't believe you said that . . ." Even now as I recount the anecdote, I find myself breathing a sigh of relief, realizing again as I replay the scene in my mind that Abe's words and those of his classmates that followed were more powerful than mine could ever have been in countering Rachel's stereotypical notions regarding Native Americans.

When I saw the students' final presentations and combed back through the data with my original question in mind, I discovered that yes, they *could* go it alone, even during uncomfortable moments, providing a strong foundation had been laid for individual readerly responses, open-ended discussion, and student-directed projects prior to the workshops. I also discovered that student choice and critical reading were not either-or propositions. Even though I had yet to hear the terms *book club* and *literature circle* at this point in my teaching, that's what I was moving toward.

## Book Clubs at Last

Ironically, that same spring, I had the opportunity to read *The Book Club Connection,* by Susan McMahon and Taffy Raphael (1997). Suddenly, I had a name in *book club* and a theoretical foundation for a concept I knew was working. I've used book clubs in my teaching ever since and have found them to be remarkably adaptable contexts that provide

⊛ opportunities for student choice in texts and response;

⊛ a corresponding increase in motivation for reading and willingness to identify oneself as a reader and a member of a reading community;

⊛ occasions for direct and indirect teaching and assessment of an array of critical interpretive strategies;

⊛ chances for students to exercise their reading independence; and

⊛ unobtrusive opportunities to conduct teacher research.

Over the past fifteen years, I've had so many book club experiences in multiple classrooms, junior high through graduate school, that you'd think I would have tired of the approach by now. But book clubs keep convincing me otherwise. While certainly not a *best practice* in the sense of being foolproof, book clubs are *consistently reliable* in approximating out-of-school contexts where readers explore texts they've chosen in the challenging but supportive company of others. So despite the detours and because of the always emerging questions, I am happy to continue my book club journey. In fact, a sixth-grade teacher summed up the feelings of many book club teachers I know, vowing, "I will never not use book clubs!"

In hopes that you too will join us on the journey, in the chapters that follow I share the many book club resources I've developed along the way, including guidelines, procedures, and an array of tools for response and assessment.

# 4

# Getting Organized

*Planning Curriculum, Assessing Needs,*
*and Matching Kids with Books*

Now that you know where my students and I have been on our book club journey, I want you to see the process I follow these days as I prepare for book clubs. Though the steps of the teaching process are as inevitably recursive as reading and writing processes, for clarity's sake in this chapter, I've ordered the procedures I use to prepare for book clubs. But it's likely that you'll be mentally multitasking, selecting books at the same time that you're considering response tools and culminating assessments. Because this isn't a cookbook, I can't promise a foolproof set of procedures. I can guarantee, however, that the resources I share are both grounded in the theory and research reviewed in Chapter 2 and informed by the experiences described in Chapter 3.

A more complex cooking metaphor is actually appropriate here, though: you can think of each section as a separate dish, but in the kitchen, as in the classroom, you should remember that you're always preparing an entire meal. In the sections that follow, I discuss the curricular, contextual, instructional, and procedural aspects of preparation, covering everything from how to choose books and plan instruction to how to set up your classroom and group students for a productive book club experience.

## Curricular and Contextual
## Aspects of Book Club Preparation

As you plan your curriculum, just where will book clubs fit? Some organize an entire semester-long class around book clubs (Faust 2005), while I and others sometimes let book clubs *become* the curriculum for a short time, a portable module that is able to fit in like a writing workshop or a thematic unit at various points in the year. Book clubs have also been the centerpiece of a thematic unit as well, scheduled at the end after students have read a number of shorter pieces. I've even threaded book clubs throughout a unit, scheduling them every Tuesday, say, and devoting a few days at the end for final book club projects. Lately, I've been using book clubs in tandem with whole-class discussion of anchor texts, the books everyone is assigned to read (see Richison, Hernandez, and Carter 2006). Scheduled for discussion every few weeks, book club books allow for reader choice but are still related thematically to the whole-class texts that anchor the curriculum. These days, most teachers I know who use book clubs alternate them with whole-class instruction and/or independent reading and writing workshops. The bottom line here is that book clubs are extremely flexible, so the first step of preparation is to think about how they will fit best into your overall curriculum.

Although the mandated curriculum refers to the set of documents and texts meant to dictate how I should run my classroom on someone else's terms, I like to think of curriculum as a *running place*, drawing on the Latin root for a *road* or *way* down which my students and I will travel together. This enacted curriculum is what my students and I actually do in the classroom on a daily basis. My job as a teacher is to be a good navigator for that road, a task that requires me to have

- a firm sense of the destination, or *goals*, since I'm familiar with the territory;

- a knowledge of *constraints* since I'll know the roads that are available for travel;

- a sense of *flexibility* that will depend on my traveling companions, the new information we'll learn, and any interesting detours we might want to pursue; and

- a spirit of *adventure* since I should always be willing to try a better route rather than see our course as fixed and rigid.

My commitment to serve as a navigator means that I'm always asking myself some basic questions when planning curriculum. I've fashioned these questions into a heuristic designed specifically for book clubs (see Figure 4.1). I recommend using the Book Club Curriculum Planning Heuristic when considering how book clubs will fit into your curriculum for a particular course. While I do urge you to consider all the categories included in the heuristic, it's unlikely that all the questions will always apply. Consequently, you should pick and choose the ones that are most relevant at a given point in time to your curriculum planning.

---

### Goals

❏ What do students need to know and be able to do as readers by the end of this unit? By the end of my course? Beyond my course at the next educational level? Outside of school? How can book clubs help them meet these overarching goals?

❏ What do the standards say? The district? My department? The students themselves?

❏ What outside assessments must I consider (e.g., standardized exams, including state assessments, AP exams, ACT, SAT, etc.)?

### Constraints

❏ What texts are best for students to read in book clubs? What texts are available? What resources can I tap to gather texts that aren't immediately available (e.g., grants, PTA funds, local libraries, etc.)?

❏ How do I allot my time so that *depth* wins out over *coverage*?

❏ What role should district book lists and community sensibilities play in my selection of book club texts?

### Flexibility

❏ Who is my student population, and what is the range of students' instructional needs?

❏ How do these needs suggest what texts and activities will work best for them in book clubs?

❏ What choices can I make available? How can I negotiate with students to determine what texts they will read and compose in book clubs?

### Adventure

❏ How do my personal reading and professional development experiences suggest new ways of approaching book clubs?

❏ How can I draw on my students' experiences and expertise as resources?

❏ What new directions would we like to try as a result?

---

FIG. 4.1. *Book Club Curriculum Planning Heuristic*

In addition to these questions, two other principles guide my curricular planning: *sequencing* and *recursivity*.

*Sequencing* of course refers to the ordering of the things—units, texts, lessons, activities, strategies, and so forth—in a deliberate and coherent fashion. When I think about sequencing, the image that comes to mind is an arrow pointing forward.

*Recursivity*, on the other hand, refers to the process of doubling back to revisit concepts, questions, or strategic processes for the purpose of deepening understanding. The image that comes to mind is a spiral, and the stance is one of inquiry.

At first glance, these images appear to contradict. How does one move forward and double back at the same time? Both images suggest an inquiry-oriented curriculum, with a starting point and a progression through a cycle of writing or learning, along with the inevitable, and potentially productive, doubling back that occurs as one composes a text or explores a question or concept.

What's the particular relevance of these images for a literature curriculum? In terms of sequencing, I'm always thinking about how I can order the texts my students read and compose so that each learning experience intentionally builds on another and prepares for an experience yet to come. As I select texts for them to read, then, I strive to move from the familiar and accessible to the less familiar and more difficult. In terms of recursivity, I ask students to revisit literary concepts or thematic questions with progressively more challenging texts.

In the following sections, I show how the aforementioned heuristic and principles informally guided the decisions Rebecca Fox and I made in planning for book clubs for the tenth graders in her pre-AP world literature classroom. Again, as you read this account, notice how we worked through every category in the Book Club Curriculum Planning Heuristic, but we considered only the questions that were most relevant for our decision making at the time.

## Adventure

As I suggested earlier, when we plan curriculum we're often holding multiple considerations in our heads at the same time, so it's difficult to say where Rebecca and I started first. It's important to note, however, that we didn't move step-by-step down the Book Club Curriculum Planning Heuristic. In fact, in some ways, I guess we actually started at the end, in the "Adventure" category, deciding to embark on a collaborative adventure as a result of a shared professional development experience. During the summer institute of the Colorado State University Writing Project (CSUWP), which I direct and to which Rebecca belongs, Rebecca volunteered her classroom to study book clubs in a whole-class setting. Rebecca had participated in book clubs herself and had implemented them in her own classroom, but she was interested in expanding the curriculum in her world literature course. In particular, she wanted to expand students' choices beyond the book room, which limited world literature to that set in remote time periods and reflecting a mainly Western European cultural focus (e.g., *The Odyssey*, *Cyrano de Bergerac*, etc.). Rebecca wondered if book clubs could provide for such an expansion. In addition, neither she nor I had tried book clubs with high school students early in the school year, so we were both curious to see how students would respond. With these inquiries in mind, we started talking texts and thus considering many of the questions listed in the heuristic under the categories of "Constraints" and "Flexibility."

## Constraints and Flexibility

Rebecca had already determined that the book room stock at her high school was insufficient to answer the questions she had in mind, but she had no school funding available for purchasing texts. Community foundation grants weren't awarded until later in the semester; however, she was able to access some CSUWP book funds with the understanding that the book sets purchased would become part of a lending library available to other CSUWP teachers once her book clubs had concluded.

As we began talking about specific titles, Rebecca's wish list included the following criteria: six contemporary world literature texts set in a variety of cultures and featuring adolescent protagonists, half of whom were female, the other half male. When considering her student population, she also knew that the texts needed to make room for the wide range of their values and perceived abilities. Since contemporary texts typically include more explicit language and situations in more accessible language than the classic texts she usually taught, and much of the community where Rebecca taught was fairly conservative, being sensitive to students' values was especially important. Instead of simply looking for texts no one could possibly find objectionable, however, we thought along a continuum of *green-light* (more likely to appeal to Rebecca's conservative students and their parents) and *yellow-light* texts (with language and circumstances a little more explicit). Even though this class was pre-AP,

Rebecca also knew from the first quarter that the population was not as academically homogeneous as the course title suggested, so she also wanted to make sure that we had a good mix of texts, ranging from more accessible to more challenging.

Working from colleagues' suggestions, book lists on the website of the Young Adult Library Services Association, reviews posted by adolescent readers on websites such as www.teenreads.com, www.guysread.com, and online bookstore websites, and our own knowledge of books, Rebecca and I were able to compile a list of texts that she felt were appropriate for her students' maturity levels and that were challenging to varying degrees. During book talks prior to forming book clubs, we read excerpts aloud and discreetly, but frankly, explained the subject matter and circumstances, language, and structural challenges (e.g., multiple narrators, parallel story lines) that students could expect to find in each text. In this way, we were able to respect students' preferences, and they were able to opt out of texts they might feel uncomfortable reading and discussing in the public forum of a book club or that might be more of an academic challenge than they were ready to take.

## Goals

Somewhere in the midst of all these discussions, Rebecca and I also discussed her instructional goals for book clubs and the instructional sequence that had preceded them. At the start of school, most students were comfortable making personal connections to and evaluations of literary texts, but a key objective in the pre-AP curriculum at her school was helping students learn to analyze texts more critically. Consequently, Rebecca spent much of the six weeks prior to our first book club meeting gearing her instruction toward Colorado state language arts standard six, part of which focuses on "knowing and using literary terminology" (Colorado Department of Education 1995).

Rebecca had laid a careful conceptual foundation before the book clubs began: students knew the literary terminology for analyzing texts and had practiced applying it to accessible texts (namely short stories) in numerous contexts (namely through independent written responses and small-group and whole-class discussions). Planning with sequencing and recursivity in mind, Rebecca was thus reasonably confident that students were prepared to give self-regulated discussions a try by the time book clubs rolled around. She also hoped that book clubs would give students the opportunity to make progressively more independent interpretive decisions about literary texts.

Rebecca was equally determined to help students see that reading could be enjoyable and fulfilling. On the graffiti wall at the front of her classroom, she regularly posed thought-provoking questions on butcher paper (e.g., "Why do we read literature?") and encouraged students to answer using colored markers. Both of us felt that book clubs would help students arrive at some authentic answers to such questions by allowing them to discuss literature in a context used by experienced readers outside of school.

Finally, as she considered external goals, Rebecca also knew that the standardized tests students would take in the spring would require them to demonstrate close reading skills, as would the AP English exams many students would take in subsequent years. On both exams, students would also have to justify their interpretations through analysis of textual evidence, and Rebecca wanted to ensure that they were prepared to do so. As we considered how to meet Rebecca's personal instructional goals and prepare students for standardized assessment, we designed response tools and a culminating project that would further develop their abilities to ground their independent interpretations in the text, discussed later in this chapter.

As we prepared for the first book club experiences Rebecca's students would have in her classroom, the Book Club Curriculum Planning Heuristic provided a good starting point for our decisions. Attending to the questions in the heuristic that were relevant for Rebecca's planning at the time helped ensure that book clubs were more than just an isolated activity or a nice break in the school year. In the end, book clubs were a meaningful part of her overall curricular sequence because they built on students' prior experiences in her class while at the same time preparing them for what was to follow within and beyond her classroom.

## Instructional Aspects of Book Club Preparation

As the previous process suggests, deciding how book clubs will fit into your overall curriculum brings up yet another set of more specific questions that will ultimately guide the instruction you provide through book clubs:

◈ How will I assess what students are learning both during book clubs and by the end of a particular book?

◈ How do I choose and acquire books?

In the next two sections, I outline the thinking processes involved in answering these questions and provide some resources to guide your thinking.

## Considering Assessment from the Start

It may seem peculiar to talk about assessment in a chapter devoted to book club preparation, but "end points suggest pathways" for teaching and learning (Smagorinsky 2002, 84). Just as having a map helps you select the most advantageous route for getting to your final destination, knowing how you (or others) will assess students at the end of a book club influences the texts and instructional tools you will select to monitor and ensure their progress along the way. You've already heard how Rebecca kept external assessments in mind as we selected the response tools her students would use for book clubs, but I want to offer another example here of how assessment functioned as a planning tool in a junior high classroom.

Stan McReynolds decided his seventh-grade language arts students were ready for book clubs in February, just one month away from the state standardized tests. Because of his district's emphasis on standards and the importance of showing improvement on these tests, Stan had developed a chart to help him see at a glance how he was addressing standards throughout the year. The chart listed his instructional units down the left side of the page and state standards across the top. At the beginning of each unit, Stan identified the standards he would use to guide his planning, and at the end of each unit, he went back to the chart and checked off those he had actually managed to address. "This keeps me honest," Stan explained as we discussed which standards the upcoming book clubs would need to address.

That February, the chart, coupled with Stan's classroom observations, suggested that his students still needed to work on predicting and inferring, skills that would most certainly be assessed on the upcoming standardized test. Because Stan's primary concern was preparing students for this test, to be administered in a few short weeks, he decided not to plan a formal assessment of his own for book clubs. Rather, he wanted to offer a set of texts and response tools that would provide an ongoing gauge of students' development of these skills and help him determine how much, if any, extra attention he might need to devote to reteaching.

Stan also had a good sense of his students' learning styles by this point in the year. Because he had determined that many of them had a preference

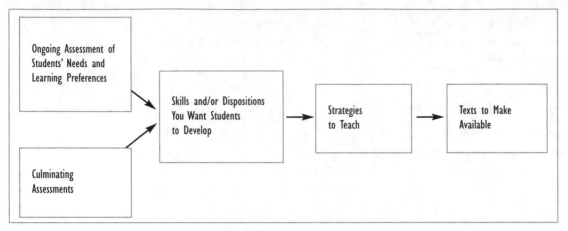

FIG. 4.2 *How assessment drives instruction*

for visual learning, he had already developed a reading log that combined icons with writing in students' responses to texts (e.g., students drew an eyeball and then wrote about something they noticed during reading). But for book clubs, Stan and I worked together to design additional response tools that would capitalize on students' proclivity for visualization while specifically focusing on prediction and inference skills. Stan also wanted students to read texts that would lend themselves to the application of these skills, such as mysteries and historical fiction. The all-boy group I worked with decided to read some short stories by Edgar Allan Poe and Art Spiegelman's *Maus*.

As Figure 4.2 illustrates, *assessing students' immediate needs and learning preferences* as readers and *recognizing how students would be evaluated* at the end of the book club sequence helped Stan determine which *skills and dispositions* he should focus on during book clubs. These in turn suggested the *ongoing response tools* we would need to design and the *texts* he would make available. In this way, identifying end points indeed suggested pathways.

Like Stan, you'll need to assess students' immediate needs as readers as well as identify the tasks they'll be expected to complete by the end of the book club cycle. Doing so will help you determine which response tools and texts will help them meet your instructional goals.

## Choosing and Acquiring Books

Sometimes finding just the right text to teach in a unit can be overwhelming, but looking for five to six texts at one time can seem downright impossible unless you have some strategies for narrowing your search. I've found that it helps to develop a set of criteria with four areas in mind: (1) culminating assessments, (2) external standards, (3) your own instructional goals, and (4) students' reading preferences and developmental needs.

Along these lines, I've developed the Text Selection Planning Guide to help you streamline the process and get your ideas down on paper (see Appendix A–1). Many of the questions listed at the top of the guide will look familiar because I alluded to them when I discussed curricular planning in more general terms. This tool, however, zooms in specifically on choosing texts. So that you can see how I use the guide to help me select book club texts for a particular course, take a look at Figure 4.3, a sample I completed for Teaching Reading, a required course I teach to English education students at Colorado State University. Before you take a look at the guide, though, it will be helpful to understand a bit about the course and how I incorporate book clubs in it.

The preservice teachers enrolled in Teaching Reading learn to design strategic reading instruction, but because they are at different points in their licensure program, many of them have minimal teaching experience. While helpful, field experiences only go so far because students are still guests in their cooperating teachers' classrooms. This means they often plan in a vacuum with only their hazy (and usually nostalgic) memories of themselves as secondary readers to inform their curricular planning. While I've always used book clubs in Teaching Reading, students usually read professional literature oriented toward theory, research, and teaching methods. One semester, however, I decided I also wanted preservice teachers to experience book clubs as their students might when reading fiction.

So I had the idea that I could use book clubs to kill two birds with one stone. Students would read young adult novels narrated by adolescents who commented on their school experiences in some way. Students would then create a Body Biography, described in detail in Chapter 6, as a sort of visual case study to analyze their respective narrator as an adolescent reader and to consider the teaching implications if that narrator were actually a student in their class. In the process my students would learn more about grounding their curricular decisions in the everydayness of adolescent readers' lives while experiencing firsthand some texts and tools they could use later in their own classrooms.

But of all the young adult novels I could teach, which ones would work best? The Sample Text Selection Planning Guide reflects my thinking and lists the texts I wound up choosing as a result (see Figure 4.3).

| | Assessments | Standards | My Instructional Goals | Students' Preferences and Needs |
|---|---|---|---|---|
| **Questions I Need to Consider** | *What major assessments will students encounter at the end of this book club? At the end of my course?* | *What standards should/could I address through book clubs?* | *What exactly do I want students to get out of book clubs?* <br><br> *How should the texts be linked together (e.g., by theme, genre, historical period, common focus or content, author, literary style, etc.)?* | *What content and text features will my students consider engaging?* <br><br> *What immediate student needs do I need to consider?* |
| **My Answers** | 1. Body Biography <br><br> 2. Assessment Portfolio (a set of lesson plans based on the needs of adolescent readers) <br><br> 3. Licensure Exam | 1. *Knowledge of Students:* Accomplished ELA teachers systematically acquire a sense of their students as individual language learners. <br><br> 2. *Instructional Resources:* Accomplished ELA teachers select, adapt, and create curricular resources that support active student exploration of literature and language processes. <br><br> (from National Board Certification Standards for English Language Arts [ELA] Teachers) | 1. I want them to learn how to plan reading instruction with the whole student in mind. <br><br> 2. I want them to have firsthand experiences with a young adult text, an instructional approach (i.e., book clubs), and a nontraditional assessment (i.e., Body Biography) that they can use in their own classrooms. | 1. Students are likely to engage with first-person narrators who use voices that seem to be authentically adolescent. <br><br> 2. Many of these students will have taken a course in young adult literature or will be taking one concurrently. Because that course takes a literary approach to YA texts and this one takes a pedagogical one, they'll need help with thinking of these texts as case studies. |
| **Resulting Criteria** | Strong protagonist who discusses reading and/or school | Fully developed protagonist who articulates a range of intellectual, emotional, and social needs | Young adult novel with a protagonist complex enough to elicit discussion and analysis | Protagonist with an engaging and authentic adolescent voice that lends herself or himself to case study analysis |
| **Texts That Come to Mind** | *Catcher in the Rye*, J. D. Salinger <br><br> *The Perks of Being a Wallflower*, Stephen Chbosky | | *Imani All Mine*, Connie Porter <br><br> *Catalyst*, Laurie Halse Andersen | |
| **Methods of Securing Books** | • Book room <br> • Student purchase with bookstore discount <br> • Department, school, or district textbook monies <br> • Beg and borrow (school and local libraries) <br> • Grants or partnerships (university, professional organizations, PTO, etc.) <br> • Donations (local businesses, community foundations, etc.) <br> • Other _____ | | | |

Note: Completed for *Teaching Reading,* a licensure course for preservice teachers at Colorado State University

FIG. 4.3 *Sample Text Selection Planning Guide*

When you're searching for possible titles, websites can be an invaluable resource. As I mentioned earlier, when Rebecca Fox and I were planning for her book clubs, we cruised websites designed specifically for adolescent readers. Also helpful are books that group books by theme and category, like *Teenplots: A Booktalk Guide to Use with Readers Ages 12–18* (Gillespie and Naden 2003) and *Good Books Lately: The One-Stop Resource for Book Groups and Other Greedy Readers* (Moore and Stevens 2004), which I describe later. After you've selected texts, acquiring copies can also be a challenge. Because you need only a small number of texts for each book club, however, it's often easier than coming up with the twenty-five to thirty copies you would need if you were teaching one text to the entire class. At the bottom of the Text Selection Planning Guide, I've listed six common sources, which teachers often use in combination.

First, though, it helps to determine what, if any, common thread you want to use to unify book club texts. As the second question in the "Instructional Goals" column of the Text Selection Planning Guide indicates, books might be linked by a theme, genre, historical time period, author, or literary style, for instance. In my Teaching Reading class, the common thread was young adult narrators whose school experiences somehow figured into the story. If your common thread allows you to feature texts from a wide range of time periods, you can sometimes find books in the book room at your school, even if it's been a while since the stock has been refurbished. In the previous chapter, I described how a thematic focus on rebels, trailblazers, and scapegoats meant I was able to find all four book club texts in the book room (*The Color Purple, One Flew over the Cuckoo's Nest, The Scarlet Letter,* and *A Yellow Raft on Blue Water*).

Depending on school demographics, student purchase is sometimes another option. Bookstore managers often offer a substantial educators' discount (usually 20 to 25 percent) and will order books in bulk so that your students don't have to pay the shipping. If the book you're teaching is a classic, you should also check to see if it's stocked by Dover Thrift Press, which sells paperbacks of many frequently taught texts for $2.00 to $3.00 per copy. Coupled with a bookstore discount, the price can be as low as $1.50, a cost almost every student can afford. Used book stores are another option, of course.

Department, school, or district funds are also sometimes available if you state a convincing rationale (it's always worth a try!), but you can also beg and borrow from school and local libraries. Finally, with advance planning, you can write grants; propose partnerships with local universities, professional organizations like your NCTE (National Council of Teachers of English) affiliate or writing project, or parent-teacher organizations; or solicit donations from local businesses or community foundations.

## Procedural Aspects of Book Club Preparation

One of the chief benefits of book clubs is the element of choice they provide, as I argue in Chapter 2, but these choices aren't limited to students, nor to texts. Even after your curricular and instructional decisions have helped you determine a menu of book club texts, you still need to figure out how to match the right kids with the right books. I've found the following procedures to be helpful as I consider these questions:

◈ How do I help students choose books?

◈ How do I group students in book clubs?

### Matching Kids with Books

When I asked sophomores from Rebecca Fox's class to explain to me how they chose their book club books, they said it was important that they weren't "deceived" into choosing the wrong book. Intrigued by this word choice, I asked for further explanation. Students went on to say that they needed to know what they were getting into before they "commited" to a book. In other words, for Rebecca's students at least, choosing a book was almost as important as deciding whom they might want to go out with, and they were uniformly opposed to the blind date.

Students' comments reminded me once again that reading is a relational act, especially when choice is involved. All of us have no doubt had the experience of growing into the arranged marriage as we read, that is, learning to love an assigned book that we probably wouldn't have chosen ourselves. But if choice is at the heart of book clubs, Rebecca's students were right. They could be wooed, but going in, they wanted to be informed. In the role of matchmakers, teachers can help by introducing students to the range of available choices and allowing students some time to get acquainted before they actually commit to a single book.

### Preparing Book Talks

A few days before a book club cycle, I begin the introduction process with book talks to "stimulate reading and a love of literature through delivering tantalizing, seductive introductions to books" (Gillespie 2003, xiii). It's helpful to know about three key elements when planning formal book talks: your readers, books in general, and several book talk resources (Gillespie 2003).

Presumably, you already will have drawn on your knowledge of readers and books in narrowing down your book club choices, but even when you're familiar with all the books, planning five to six book talks at once go can be inordinately time-consuming when you consider that for each book talk you'll need to provide a brief overview of the book, read a few key passages so that students can get a sense of the narrator's voice and author's style, and offer any ancillary information that might help readers make an informed choice. And that's where knowledge of book talk resources comes in handy. Next, I offer some resources to help with your book talk planning.

**GATHERING MATERIAL FOR OVERVIEWS** In the interest of time, I suggest that you draw on external resources when preparing overviews for book talks, even when introducing books you have read several times. Obviously, you can check out the book jacket, but you should also ask your school librarian about the resources he or she consults when ordering new books or preparing book talks. For instance, books such as *Teenplots* and *Good Books Lately*, mentioned earlier, provide brief summaries of contemporary texts. Online bookstores also provide descriptions that are typically about a paragraph in length, just about right for book talks. If you scroll down the webpage that describes the book, you will also find more detailed reviews from published sources like *Booklist* and *Publisher's Weekly* as well as reader reviews that can be more or less helpful. The published reviews often include information about awards, age appropriateness, and so on. Finally, to find out how willing adolescent readers have responded to particular books, you can also search websites like www.teenreads.com.

I usually cut and paste summaries for all the books I'm introducing into a one-page Word document, but I don't read them verbatim during book talks. Doing so would be about as compelling as reading a personal ad aloud rather than informally describing a potential date I'm trying to arrange for my friend. Just as setting someone up demands firsthand information rather than hearsay, your students will want to see your personal connection with a book. The overviews you gather from outside sources thus make useful notes to speak from, but in the end, book talks must be conversational. Consequently, I suggest that you highlight main characters and events you want to mention and do your best to maintain eye contact with students as you move quickly from one book to the next.

**FINDING KEY PASSAGES TO READ ALOUD** Books like *Teenplots* often recommend passages for book talking, but you should also trust your own judgment in choosing representative segments of the book that your students are likely to find compelling. Think of the last movie trailer you saw. If by the end, you felt as if there was no point left in seeing the movie, filmmakers showed too much. If, however, you got enough of a sense of the story that you wanted to keep watching, the trailer was just right. Likewise, in selecting a passage or two to read during book talks, your goal is to intrigue, not to inundate, to represent without revealing too much. Readers should still feel as if promising territory awaits their own discovery.

Along these lines, you will most often choose passages from the beginning or first half of the book, so you aren't giving too much away. These passages should contain one or more of the following features. They should

* introduce main characters

* provide a glimpse into important relationships

* foreshadow key events

* preview central conflicts

* pose a compelling question or dilemma

* capture the narrator's voice

* give a sense of the author's style

* provide a feel for the setting, especially in the case of fantasy or science fiction, where it is often inextricable from the plot

Remember Rebecca's students' advice: readers don't want to be deceived, but rather to know what they're getting themselves into before they fully commit to a book.

As an aside, their advice is likely to be partially grounded in the mistake I made when book talking Aidan Chambers' *Postcards from No Man's Land* for Rebecca's class. The book features parallel story lines. One is set in the present and involves, among other things, the narrator Jacob's conflicting feelings about his sexuality. The other is set during World War II and involves a relationship between Jacob's soldier grandfather and the young woman who cares for his injuries. Even though during my book talk, I explained both story lines much as I have here, I read only one key passage, which involved the second story line. The students who chose the book were disappointed to find that it was less of the plot-driven wartime novel they had expected and more of a study in characters. It's important, then, that the passages you choose to read during book talks do have a representative quality, and if more than one story line or point of view is featured, you may want to read an excerpt from each.

**IDENTIFYING ANCILLARY INFORMATION** To round out a book talk, consider what else your students may want to know about a book. Some will be interested in information about the author that is especially relevant to the book, such as that S. E. Hinton wrote *The Outsiders* when she was sixteen and based much of the plot on her own high school experiences in Tulsa, Oklahoma. They may also want to know about awards the book has received and the lists it has made, as well as the nature of these awards and lists. A book's publishing history may also be relevant here. For instance, my students have been interested to know that Louis Sachar's *Holes* won the National Book Award as well as the Newbery. It was also marketed as a book for adults in England, thus suggesting the book's range of appeal. Such information is often included in the online bookstores' summaries I mentioned earlier. There and on sites like www.teenreads.com and www.guysread.com you can also find pithy reviews you may want to quote.

Finally, students may appreciate knowing about a book's heads-up traits, such as unusual treatment of structure or genre, multiple narrators, strong language, graphic or explicit scenes, and so forth. When I share this information during book talks, I do so not to be censorious or dissuasive, but to prepare students for what they're about to read. Sometimes, in fact, this information serves an instructive purpose or even winds up making the book more marketable. Adolescent readers profit from introductions to unfamiliar genres as well. For instance, students reading Karen Hesse's *Out of the Dust* will need to know that the novel is written in the form of free-verse poems. If they were reading *Monster*, they'd need to know that Walter Dean Myers combines a number of genres in telling the story.

Experience has also taught me that the peculiar nature of the book club context makes it important that students know in advance if a book contains language or subject matter they might feel uncomfortable discussing with their peers. In the continuum of private and public reading experiences in school, book clubs exist somewhere in the middle. It's one thing to write about a controversial scene in a reading log that only your teacher will read. In whole-class discussion, a reticent student can easily disappear while the braver students carry on, and no one but the teacher need be the wiser. But when the person on your right turns to you during book club and asks you what you think, it's far more difficult to hide. In this sense, book clubs are typically more intimate than whole-class discussions. This doesn't mean that you need to go into great detail or read an explicit scene aloud during a book talk. But being frank with students by simply explaining that a book includes some graphic or explicit elements gives them the heads-up they need so that they can investigate the book further before committing to reading it in a book club setting.

## Delivering Book Talks and Acquainting Students with Books

This past summer during a dinner party I was hosting, I recommended *The Kite Runner,* by Khaled Hosseini, to my friend Karen, who had insisted earlier in the year that I read Nazar Afisi's *Reading Lolita in Tehran.* "Oh, I just finished a book you have to read! It's about a boy growing up in Afghanistan who moves to America, and I really think you'll love it. It was a little slow for me at first, but once I got to a certain point, I couldn't put it down. Here, let me just show you . . ." And then I temporarily abandoned the rest of my dinner guests to fetch the book and foist it upon Karen. She flipped through the pages before agreeing that it was a book she needed to read. Although the book talks I give my students are more detailed than this, they are almost as conversational and have the same result.

Here again, the matchmaker's goal when delivering book talks is to introduce students to a potential new "bibliomate." They will want to see the actual books you recommend, so you should hold them up as you're describing them and then display them on the chalk tray or a table near the front of the room. After book talks, students will also need some time to hold the books, take a closer look on their own, read the covers, skim through the pages, and decide which match is right. If you already have book sets available in your room, students can do so immediately following book talks and make their decisions in pretty short order. If they are purchasing books or you're still in the process of gathering, however, students will need a few more days to browse through your available copies. You can also encourage them to "visit" the books at online bookstore websites, which often have "see inside" features that allow previewing of sample pages.

## Determining Book Choices and Grouping Students

Determining students' final choices and grouping them in book clubs go hand in hand. The process is admittedly unscientific, and yes, some students will try to outsmart the system, but they usually do no real harm. Three key considerations are (1) honoring students' book preferences, (2) balancing the size of groups, and (3) trusting your intuitions about social dynamics.

The first part of the process is straightforward. I simply ask students to list their top three choices of book club books and explain that even though they all won't get their first choice, I will do my best to grant one of the top three. Depending on the age of students or on the context of the book club (i.e., whether it is in class or outside of class), I sometimes also ask students to list one person they would like to have in their book club. I've discovered that with older students, getting the book they want usually takes priority over working with particular classmates. This is especially true for in-class book clubs. With younger students or students in out-of-class book clubs, however, social needs tend to prevail, making group membership more important. Either way, unless you have an unlimited number of book sets, students' text choices should be your starting point if you want to balance the size of groups and make sure that your entire menu of books will be read.

Your next step is sorting students' lists as you might a deck of playing cards, granting as many first choices as possible while keeping the number of students in each group approximately the same. In a class of thirty students choosing among six books, for instance, your goal is to make six groups of five students each. Rarely will a class divide themselves evenly, and so the balancing act begins. Typically, about midway through the process, groups begin to emerge according to reading preferences. If some students have lobbied hard for a certain book (and trust me, some will), you may decide in the previous example to allow three groups of five, one of six, and one of four, but I've found four to six members to be the optimum size for a book club. More than six per group, and it's easy for someone to get lost in the crowd. Fewer than four, and it's difficult to sustain conversation if someone is absent.

To maintain balanced numbers, it usually becomes necessary at this point to consider some students' second and third choices. Here, too, is when your intuition about the social dynamics among students kicks into play. All I can say in this area is that you need to trust your knowledge of your students. Keep in mind their stated preferences for peers with whom they would like to work, their work ethic in prior groups, and your own sense of students' interactive tendencies. When several students lobby to work together, I usually go along, remembering that even as an experienced reader, I'm more likely to take interpretive risks when I trust others in my group. But I make sure that students understand one condition: working with one's friends is an earned privilege that can be revoked if the group ceases to be productive or constructive. In terms of students' interactive tendencies, the following questions also run through my mind as I'm grouping students into book clubs:

- How might I match the student who tends to dominate discussions with another student who can hold her own?

- Could I match a more reserved student with an empathic student who invites the ideas of others?

- How can I balance students' needs for intellectual challenge and emotional safety?

Your answers will of course depend on your teaching context, but I want to add another important question here in regard to social dynamics: *What roles should gender balance and class and racial diversity play?*

As I engage in routine and seemingly apolitical tasks, like grouping students into book clubs, Susan Hynds' (1997) research helpfully complicates my choices. In her study of junior high teacher Meg's urban language arts classroom, Hynds discovered that the ideal of a democratic classroom is just that—an ideal—since students' social interactions within classrooms generally reflect the social inequities that exist beyond classrooms. When Meg's vision of her classroom as "one happy family" fell through, she allowed students to work in "affinity groups" made up of peers with whom they felt comfortable collaborating (265). While students clearly gained social and academic power and confidence through their experiences in these groups, both Meg and Hynds were troubled that membership tended to be divided along racial and gender lines.

Although she does not recommend that Meg should have broken up the affinity groups or attempted to integrate them, Hynds' research helped her realize that "teachers have the responsibility to at least point out racial or gender segregation, *especially* if it is the result of personal choice. Although affinity groups may be a necessary stepping stone to a cohesive classroom community, there are times when students might be nudged into collaborations with other students that they might not pursue on their own" (265). This, of course, is no easy task, but I try to remember Hynds' advice that "the literacy classroom can and must be an arena for exploring the social and political dynamics of the larger world, and . . . the teacher often bears the responsibility for initiating such explorations" (266). The mindful formation of book clubs can certainly be a place to help students begin this important task.

The curricular, instructional, and procedural aspects of book club preparation I've mentioned in this chapter are important for setting up book clubs so that they will run as smoothly as possible from the start. In the next chapter, I explain how it's also important to help students prepare for and sustain substantive book club discussions. There, you'll find lots of response tools designed to prompt their conversations, resources for keeping track of them, and suggestions for what to do with yourself while students are doing all the talking.

# 5

# Time to Talk

*Preparing for Meaningful Book Club Conversations*

As you've probably gathered by now, good conversation is the hallmark of the effective book club. As students interpret texts collaboratively, they become more independent, engaged readers in the process. Substantive book club conversations are unlikely to happen, however, just because you've let kids choose the books they want to read and placed them in groups of four to talk about them. While the previous chapter focused on teacher preparation, this chapter offers guidelines and practical resources for helping students prepare for and sustain their book club discussions.

## Before the First Book Club:
## Norms, Reading Schedules, and Response Tools

As I mentioned in Chapter 2, in addition to all the procedural preparations of book club, kids have to be prepared to go it alone in classroom discussions if they don't have a more experienced reader in their midst, such as a classroom volunteer. Even if they do, you'll still need to give some advance thought to helping your students develop and observe norms for productive book club discussions.

Some of this preparation takes place during classroom norming, the instructional groundwork you've laid previously to help students understand how free-flowing discussions work. Because student-led discussions of literature tend to mirror the teacher-led discussions that precede them (Marshall, Smagorinsky, and Smith 1995) students need scaffolding to help them bridge the gap between what they can accomplish with assistance in a teacher-led discussion and what they can handle alone in student-led discussions.

Rebecca Fox's sophomore English classroom illustrates how this gradual release of control can take place. Rebecca began the year modeling her expectations in teacher-led, whole-class discussions, and then she moved her students into structured small groups, using discussion questions she provided. Finally Rebecca allowed them to carry on discussions entirely by themselves in small groups, until her students were able to sustain Socratic seminars for an entire fifty-minute class with no intervention by her beyond reminding students of guidelines at the beginning of the class period. As a result, students were highly prepared for book club discussions after only about six weeks of school.

In my own high school classroom, I followed a similar pattern, devoting explicit attention to my expectations for how small-group discussions ought to run and making sure that students had the tools to meet these expectations. Although I didn't use teacher-designed study questions after my first year of teaching, I taught students early in the year how to cull questions and topics from their reading journals and then use these to guide their small-group discussions. In both Rebecca's classes and my own, I observed how these experiences established implicit norms that students tended to follow in book club discussions as well.

I again learned the hard way, however, that implicit modeling sometimes isn't enough. Before the first book club meeting, students need direct attention to matters experienced readers take in stride, such as respecting others' viewpoints, using a reading schedule to pace oneself, and responding to texts strategically.

## Setting Book Club Norms and Making a Reading Schedule

In addition to reminding students of the norms already in place in your classroom, I also recommend asking students to set their own norms for their individual book clubs. As I learned when studying small-group literature discussions in my twelfth-grade classroom, students will not always play nice with one another, even when the teacher is browsing around the room to answer questions and monitor behavior. Small groups can be extraordinarily supportive contexts, but they can also perpetuate the inequitable social relationships that are already in place before students darken the classroom door (Smagorinsky and O'Donnell-Allen 1998a). That's why asking students to establish rules for respectful interaction at the start of book clubs and then to occasionally evaluate how well they are following them is a must.

This process can be as informal as asking students to make a list of goals and guidelines for how they want their book club to run. These should be in students' own language, and everyone should record his or her own copy for future reference and share a copy with you as well. Nowadays, I ask students to spend their first book club session establishing a reading schedule and completing the more detailed handout Our Book Club Goals and Ground Rules (see Appendix B–1). This handout asks students to imagine the ideal book club and set goals to achieve it. Students sign these agreements, and I make copies for everyone and keep a copy for myself.

One group of Rebecca's sophomores, who had named themselves the Petrified Pandas, came up with the following list of goals and ground rules:

## Goals

1. Everyone enjoys the book.

2. Everyone follows the ground rules.

3. No one talks too much.

4. We learn from the discussion every time.

## Ground Rules

1. Everyone participates.

2. Respect everyone's ideas and opinions.

3. Always be prepared (bring book, have pages read).

4. The discussion will start with questions.

5. If not following ground rules, one will not be allowed to talk for five minutes.

The goals and guidelines students establish for their book clubs are always interesting, but observing how they hold one another to them is even more interesting. Some groups establish consequences for students who don't keep up with the reading, make plans for emailing written responses in advance if they have to be absent on book club day, or create guidelines to ensure that students have equal airtime during discussion. Devoting explicit attention to norming helps students establish community and understand their expectations for one another, and it greatly reduces policing during book clubs on my part. Because I review students' norms before the first book club session, I'm not only able to troubleshoot and suggest revisions of any rules that sound unreasonable but also able to redirect students to the set of rules *they* agreed upon, should anyone get off track during book club. About halfway through a book club cycle, I also like to ask students to do a quick self-assessment on a half sheet of paper, revisiting their original goals and guidelines and then rating their participation as individuals as well as a group.

In addition to establishing norms prior to the first book club session, students also need to determine the reading schedule they will follow in order to be prepared for each book club. I ask students to follow these steps:

- Write down the total number of pages in your book.

- Divide this number by the total number of book club sessions (e.g., 200 pages ÷ 4 book club sessions = 50 pages per session). This will give you a rough estimate of the number of pages you'll need to read in order to be prepared for each book club.

- Now look at where these breaks actually fall in your book. Since they probably won't occur naturally at the end of chapters, agree as a group on how to divide the segments.

- Write down the page number you'll need to have finished beside the date for each book club session.

Students can record this information in a place where they won't lose it, such as a planner or class notebook, but my students have more luck following the schedule when they record it on a bookmark, like the Sticky Notes Bookmark I describe later in the chapter.


## Response Tools That Encourage Exploratory Discourse

As I said in the last chapter, the response tools you choose for students should align with their immediate needs as readers as well as the assessments you'll expect them to complete once book clubs are finished. Since discussion is the primary means through which they'll meet these ends, these response tools should also get students talking. The response tools that follow are meant to help students learn to independently and collaboratively interpret texts through "exploratory," as opposed to "final draft," discourse (Barnes 1992).

Exploratory talk involves "groping towards meaning" (Barnes 1992, 28) as speakers tentatively attempt to interpret, explain, or evaluate ideas, which may in turn be clarified or elaborated upon by other group members. Contestants on the television quiz show *Who Wants to Be a Millionaire?* use exploratory talk to think through the choices aloud. Sometimes, they even phone a friend to talk over the choices further. Exploratory discourse can be *catalytic* in that it can cause both speakers and listeners to change their minds and arrive at new meanings. Eventually, though, quiz contestants must settle on final answers. Once they do, they've transitioned into *final-draft* talk. Final-draft statements offer resolution to thought in final form, representing one's final word on a subject. You use language in an exploratory manner when you write, doodle, or talk through an idea to figure out what you are trying to say, and you use final-draft talk when you state a claim with confidence.

English teachers face a perennial dilemma. We know our secondary classrooms may represent our students' last best chance for experiencing effective literacy practices, such as exploratory discourse, while they engage with reading and writing, yet we may also face criticism by some parents, administrators, and more traditional colleagues as favoring intellectually soft and touchy-feely discussion rather than preparing students for the next level or the next standardized test, which inevitably involves more analysis, more abstraction, and more formal writing. How do we engage students and maintain rigor at the same time? Must we sacrifice one goal for the other?

A voluminous body of research concludes that "students learn literature best in classrooms that encourage substantive and personal student response to literature in both classroom interaction and writing" (Nystrand 1997, 105). Book clubs promote a range of exploratory discourse, offer a theoretically sound approach to meeting the needs of adolescent readers, supported by a solid body of research (reported in Chapter 2), and help students understand how reading, speaking, and composing can be mutually supportive processes.

Additional research details the specific benefits of exploratory discourse; it:

- deepens students' understanding of texts by requiring them to justify their interpretations and extend one another's thinking (Barnes

1992; Barnes and Todd 1977; Smagorinsky and O'Donnell-Allen 1998b);

- helps them learn to think for themselves by *constructing* literary meaning rather than merely *receiving* it (Hillocks 1989; Nystrand 1997; Wells and Chang-Wells 1992);

- helps students learn to listen, converse, and respectfully disagree, given an atmosphere of mutual respect (O'Donnell-Allen and Smagorinsky 1999; Smagorinsky and O'Donnell-Allen 1998b); and

- allows students to use a range of literacy practices in active, integrated, and meaningful ways (Smith and Wilhelm 2002; Wells 2001; Wilhelm 1997).

To help readers successfully explore texts individually through writing and visualization prior to a book club meeting, I recommend using any of the ten response tools summarized in the Top Ten Toolbox chart found in Figure 5.1. The chart explains at a glance what the tools are, why they work, and when to use them. If I've described how a tool originated earlier in the book, I refer you to a previous chapter and provide only a brief description and rationale following the chart. Otherwise, I provide the origin, description, and rationale of each new tool. Reproducible handouts for all of the response tools are located in Appendix C.

For continuity's sake and to help students fully develop the emphasized strategies, I usually ask them to use a single response tool for an entire book club cycle. Students use their individual responses to fuel book club discussion.

## The Top Ten Response Tools

### ,/?/! (The Punctuation Prompt)

I developed the Punctuation Prompt response tool as I thought about how common punctuation marks might be used as a heuristic to prompt students to think provisionally about a section of the text before discussing it in book club. Students select and respond to three different passages or central ideas, using each of the three punctuation marks as a heading. Under the *comma* heading, they explain why a particular passage made them stop and think. Under the *question mark* heading, they list a question they have about another passage or explain what it made them wonder

| Strategy | What It Is | | |
|---|---|---|---|
| ,!?!! **(Punctuation Prompt)** | A strategy that requires students to identify three passages or central ideas in the text and explain how these passages or ideas:<br>(1.) gave them pause (2.) made them wonder (3.) provoked a strong reaction | | |
| **1-2-3-Predict** | A strategy that requires students to sketch three significant events that occurred in a text plus one event they predict might happen next and briefly explain their choices | | |
| **Dailies** | A four-column graphic organizer with room for individual response, discussion notes, and reader reflection | | |
| **Mind Map Reading Log** | A strategy that requires students to sketch symbols that analyze a character and then explain these symbols briefly in writing | | |
| **Picture This** | A dialogic strategy in which students sketch a scene or event from the reading on the top half of the page and then write an extended response describing its significance on the bottom half of the page | | |
| **Q & R (Quotation and Response)** | A two-column response method that requires students to critically respond to passages they've chosen, using one of the following options:<br>(1.) accept (2.) question (3.) resist (4.) reject | | |
| **Reading Log** | A two-column response method that requires students to list passages they deem significant on the left side of the page and respond to them on the right side of the page | | |
| **Real Books Letter** | An open-ended strategy written in the form of a friendly letter that includes personal response, vocabulary development, and reading reflection | | |
| **Real Questions** | An inquiry-oriented strategy that requires students to list their own questions in response to a text and begin exploring provisional answers | | |
| **Sticky Notes Bookmark** | A bookmark that combines a reading schedule and prompts to which students respond on sticky notes they attach directly to their books during reading | | |

FIG. 5.1. *Top 10 Toolbox*

| | Why It Works and When to Use It | Where to Look |
|---|---|---|
| | ,?!! (aka the Punctuation Prompt) fosters lively discussion because it prompts the kinds of provocative responses engaged readers typically have to texts. Use this strategy when you want students to consider a manageable range of intellectual and emotional responses. | Chapter 5 |
| | 1-2-3-Predict helps students trace the plot of a text by identifying significant events and inferring future outcomes. Use this strategy to teach literary techniques associated with plot (e.g., foreshadowing, inciting incident, climax, etc.) and to encourage inference. | Chapter 1 |
| | This strategy helps students learn how to take notes during reading and book club discussion and to trace the development of their literary interpretations. Use this strategy to help students reflect on their reading processes over time. | Chapter 5 |
| | This strategy helps students move beyond comprehension to more abstract levels of interpretation. Use Mind Map Reading Logs when teaching characterization, especially to reluctant writers. | Chapter 5 |
| | This strategy helps students visualize what they are reading, a commonplace skill among engaged readers. Use this strategy when focusing on setting or plot development, especially with reluctant readers and writers. | Chapter 5 |
| | This strategy requires students to defend their emotional reactions to a text through close attention to passages they select. Use Q & Rs with texts that raise big ideas, questions, and issues (i.e., those that students are likely to find thought provoking or controversial in some way). | Chapter 5 |
| | Sentence-stem prompts provide students with a range of choices and offer built-in scaffolding for those who are unfamiliar with open-ended approaches to literary response. Use Reading Logs when you want to wean students away from teacher-centered prompts (e.g., study questions) or mere summaries, for instance, at the beginning of the school year. | Chapter 3 |
| | Because of the format, students find Real Books Letters to be an accessible way to explore their ideas about a text in writing. Use this strategy when you want to strengthen voice, gain insight into students' reading processes, and encourage contextualized vocabulary development. | Chapter 3 |
| | This strategy encourages engagement through inquiry and results in substantive book club discussion as students consider questions in which they are truly invested. Use Real Questions to help students learn what constitutes a generative question as opposed to a known-answer question. | Chapter 5 |
| | Sticky Notes Bookmarks remind students of reading deadlines and allow them to respond to texts without disrupting the flow of their reading. Use this strategy to encourage reading discipline and teach various theoretical approaches to literary interpretation. | Chapter 5 |

about. Finally, under the *exclamation mark* heading, they describe how a different passage provoked a strong reaction in them as they read.

Because students can select only three passages, they are required to make some tough choices, yet the punctuation prompts ensure that they are considering a range of responses. Students inevitably choose different passages when using this response tool and as a result wind up having a substantive discussion on the most significant parts of the text.

## 1-2-3-Predict

I describe the origin of this strategy in Chapter 1. This response tool consists of four rectangles. In the first three rectangles, students sketch the three most important events in a given section of their book club book. In the space underneath each of these rectangles, they write a caption explaining the significance of the illustrated event. In the fourth rectangle, students draw a scene predicting what they think might happen in the next section of the book. The caption under this rectangle explains why this event is likely to occur.

These reading logs appeal to visually oriented students because they allow students to draw. Yet they also require students to make interpretive decisions about the text's most important events, ones that are likely to encourage meaningful book club discussion, especially when students sketch different events. The logs help students develop skills of prediction and inference and give them practice in justifying their interpretations through writing, the medium preferred on standardized tests.

## Dailies

The Dailies response tool is an adaptation of the two-column "dialectical journal" created to help students respond to a class novel (Robertson 1998). I wanted students to have a place for recording their individual responses to a text as well as those of their book club. I also wanted them to reflect on the ways their book club interaction had influenced their initial individual responses, so I added columns and prompts. Dailies were the result; the name is meant to convey my expectation that reading and responding to their book club books should become a daily routine.

This four-column graphic organizer helps students trace their evolving response to a text over time in book club. Student use the first two "What I Think" columns to respond to the text while they are reading, before the book club discussion. In the third column, "What My Book

Club Thinks," they take notes during the book club discussion. They complete the fourth column, "What I Think Now," after the book club discussion, reflecting on how it has influenced their thinking.

Not only do Dailies help students see the provisional and collaborative nature of literary interpretation, but they also emphasize how the processes of reading, writing, and discussion support one another. Because Dailies provide a fairly exhaustive record of students' thinking, complete with page numbers for future reference, my students have found them to be invaluable for culminating assessments such as analytical essays.

## Mind Map Reading Log

I developed this response tool for a book club full of seventh-grade boys who loved to draw but weren't nearly as crazy about writing (see also the Open Mind, a similar tool developed by Blau to prompt student response to poetry, cited in Strickland and Strickland 1998, 195). As you can see by the example in Figure 5.2, which I completed for "The Telltale Heart," students map a character by drawing three symbols and writing three significant words from the reading inside the character's head. Next, they make a legend for their map by explaining what their symbols represent and why they chose those words. Finally, they record three questions they still have about the reading.

The Mind Map Reading Log capitalizes on today's students' capacity for visualization, requiring them to distill their thinking about the text into just three important images and words. Because they must come to the table with three questions, students also approach the story from an inquiry-oriented perspective that virtually guarantees genuine discussion. Why the number *three*? It's not a Holy Trinity thing, I assure you. In fact, you could easily change the number if so inclined. Just be sure to keep the number small because aside from having the distilling effect I mentioned already, I've found that three feels manageable to students, even with very difficult texts.

## Picture This

The Picture This response tool is an adaptation of the Real Books Letter I described in Chapter 3. It emerged during an informal study I conducted with a class of juniors to determine why students who can read simply choose not to. Their discussion was so striking that I summarized it in the teaching journal I was keeping at the time. Because I had assigned short selections up to that point in the year, most students had been reading along cooperatively, but when I announced that it was time to begin Willa Cather's My *Antonia*, a sizable group vocally objected. The students who looked forward to starting a novel were as puzzled as I was by those who said they would rather do anything but read. In response, the rebel group of students said that reading was boring. "You aren't doing anything," I remember one boy complaining. "Why read when you can go outside and play baseball?"

"I can read a page ten times and not remember a single word," a girl added. "Even when I try to concentrate, my mind just wanders."

A student from the first group was floored. "You mean you don't see what's happening when you read?" she asked, and she went on to explain that she loved to read because it was like having her own personal movie projector inside her head. As the discussion continued, students proposed a variation on the Real Books Letter assignment (described in more detail on page 84), and the result was Picture This.

As the name implies, Picture This is designed to help students picture what they're reading. On the top half of a sheet of paper, students sketch a significant scene or image from the text and then explain its importance on the bottom half of the page. The sketch can have literal roots in the reading, or it can be more symbolic in nature, but it should lead to further discussion, and it usually does, as students discover the differences and commonalities among the movies that have been playing in their heads. This response tool has the additional benefit of helping students visualize and reflect upon their reading processes and observe those of their peers as well (Bigelow and Vokoun 2005; Smith and Wilhelm 2002).

## Q & R (Quotation and Response)

Another version of a double-entry reading log, the Q & R gives students four options for critically responding to passages that have evoked strong emotional reactions. After drawing a line down the center of the page, students record quotations in the left-hand column and then respond to them in the right-hand column. The students' first option is to pose a *question* provoked by a particular passage or the reading selection as a whole. This question is meant to spur on book club discussion, but because I also want students to use writing to explore their thinking, I ask them to try to begin working out an answer on paper. Their second option is to *accept* an idea from the reading and explain why. Students can also *resist* a passage's ideas by describing which parts of it are appealing and challenging those that

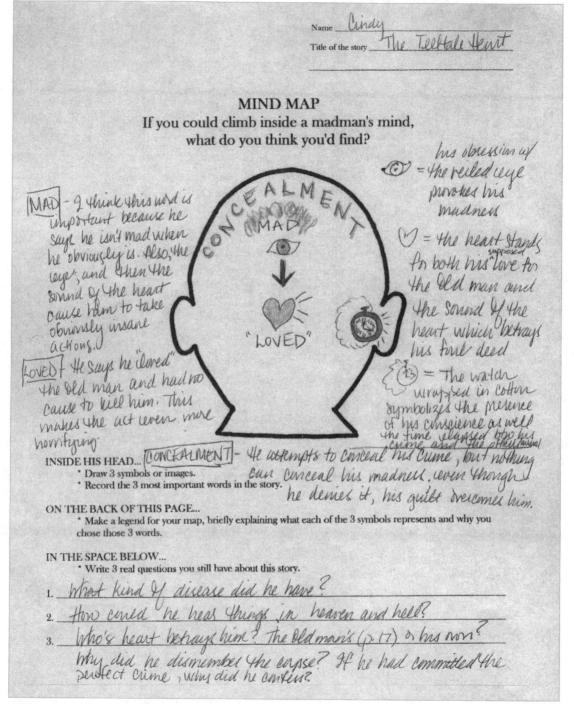

Name Cindy
Title of the story The TellTale Heart

**MIND MAP**
If you could climb inside a madman's mind,
what do you think you'd find?

CONCEALMENT

MAD
"LOVED"

MAD - I think this word is important because he says he isn't mad when he obviously is. Also, the eyes, and then the sound of the heart cause him to take obviously insane actions.

LOVED - He says he "loved" the old man and had no cause to kill him. This makes the act even more horrifying.

his obsession w/
= the veiled eye provokes his madness

= the heart stands for both his supposed love for the old man and the sound of the heart which betrays his foul deed

= The watch wrapped in cotton symbolizes the presence of his conscience as well the time elapsed b/w his crime and the other arrival

INSIDE HIS HEAD... CONCEALMENT - He attempts to conceal his crime, but nothing
   * Draw 3 symbols or images.      can conceal his madness. even though
   * Record the 3 most important words in the story.   he denies it, his guilt overcomes him.

ON THE BACK OF THIS PAGE...
   * Make a legend for your map, briefly explaining what each of the 3 symbols represents and why you chose those 3 words.

IN THE SPACE BELOW...
   * Write 3 real questions you still have about this story.

1. What kind of disease did he have?
2. How could he hear things in heaven and hell?
3. Who's heart betrays him? The Old man's (p. 17) or his own?
   Why did he dismember the corpse? If he had committed the perfect crime, why did he confess?

FIG. 5.2. Mind Map

seem unlikely. Finally, if a quotation goes against every fiber of their being, students can completely *reject* a passage and explain why.

Students usually find this strategy to be empowering. So often in schools they are asked to swallow texts whole, never questioning what a published author has to say. Q & Rs demand that they claim their readerly rights and articulate their reactions for themselves and others (speaking of rights, I urge you to take a look at the delightfully provocative Reader's Bill of Rights in Daniel Pennac's *Better than Life* [1999]). Students tend to react more strongly to books they've chosen. Unfortunately, however, they often don't know where to go beyond "I really liked this part, but I didn't like this one." Despite the fact that Q & Rs limit response options to four, this response tool works well for book clubs because the options are spread out along a continuum, so students have somewhere to go in between. Furthermore, they require students to record the specific passages that provoked their reactions, thus ensuring that discussion will be grounded in the text.

## Reading Logs

I describe the origin of this strategy in Chapter 3, but it's important to add here that this was the first response tool I tried after I gave up study questions once and for all, and I've used it ever since.

For each segment of their book club book, students divide one piece of notebook paper into two columns. In the left column, they record quotations that caught their attention while reading—lines or passages that appealed to them, confused them, made them react strongly, or really made them think. In the right column, they explain why they chose each quotation by writing questions or comments, drawing conclusions, making connections to other passages, texts, or their own experiences, and so forth.

Reading logs help students think about what they are reading while at the same time providing fodder for their book club discussions. Because these logs provide a record of students' responses throughout the text, they are also valuable preparation for their final assessments.

## Real Books Letter

In Chapter 3, I recall how my students coined the name for this strategy, but letters responding to literary texts and addressed to the teacher or peers have been around for a while. They function primarily as a written exchange in reading workshops, for example (Atwell 1998), but in book clubs, I've frequently used them to prime the conversational pump, partly because they're so very adaptable.

The format is quite basic. Students write a letter responding to, not summarizing, the assigned portion of their book club book. Although I remind students that I want to see *letters, not postcards,* I keep the length to a couple of handwritten pages, or one typed page. I remind them, "Write and think on paper in *your voice,* primarily for *your own benefit* in discovering what *you* know about this book." Because the epistolary format is so familiar, especially since the advent of email, students find Real Books Letters extremely accessible. As Anne Lamott explains, writing letters often frees writers from "the tyranny of perfectionism" (1994, 172).

Beyond that point, I include a small number of additional components according to my instructional purposes at the time. For instance, the version I've included in Appendix C–8 requires that students discuss the most important event or quotation of the section, comment on how they see the book relating to the unit theme, reflect on their reading processes, and define five interesting words in that section of the book. Regardless of the prompts you develop, it's important to keep them similarly open-ended and to leave room for students to respond in other ways as well.

## Real Questions

My former high school students get the credit for naming this response tool as well because in a discussion long ago, they distinguished between "teacher questions" and "real questions." One day when I was attempting to drum up interest about some text, students just sat there, staring into space, picking their fingernails, nodding off. No one was having any fun, and I felt great empathy for dentists who hope their clients will still like them because a reasonable person knows that filling cavities is ultimately for the patient's own good. Finally, I gave up and demanded to know what the problem was. "Do you really want to know?" an exasperated student finally asked. Well, of course I really did. "Why do you even ask questions if you already know the answers?"

His bravery got others' attention, and they went on to explain to me how very well they understood the discourse pattern peculiar to schools known as the IRE, short for initiate-respond-evaluate (Cazden 1988). Most class "discussion" follows this pattern, in which the teacher asks a question, a student answers, and the teacher in turn evaluates the response as right or wrong, good or bad, or whatever. To recognize the peculiarity of this discourse pattern to schools, imagine this pattern in another setting. Say you're standing in the supermarket checkout line and you ask the cashier, "How much are the peas?" When he answers, how ridiculous would it be if you responded, "Correct"?

There's nothing inherently wrong with teachers asking questions. But if you try to break the IRE pattern the next time you're leading a discussion, you'll find that honest-to-goodness discussion is harder to come by than you might think. In fact, my students were objecting to known-answer questions that teachers ask, wishing instead for real questions, authentic questions posed by someone who didn't already know the answer—"How much are the peas?" The Real Questions strategy is meant to get at the latter sort of questions and disrupt the IRE pattern in the process.

This strategy is so straightforward, you won't find a reproducible master for it in Appendix C. After making a more streamlined distinction between *teacher questions* and *real questions* than I just did, simply ask students to write three real questions in response to the assigned reading. Then ask them to choose *the question they care about the most* and begin working toward provisional answers to it. Remind them that if it's a real question, they probably won't arrive at any hard-and-fast answers.

This strategy helps students approach texts from a stance of inquiry. Because they are usually invested in their questions, they tend to find book club discussion satisfying. Asking students to begin considering answers to one question before a book club meeting encourages exploratory writing and helps students realize they need not depend solely on the teacher to provide all the answers. As this exploratory writing is augmented by exploratory book club discussion, students are truly involved in the coconstruction of meaning. Finally, if you ask them to periodically reflect on which questions provoked the most substantive discussion, they will learn more about the nature of generative questions as well.

## Sticky Notes Bookmarks

If I were counting down these top ten response tools David Letterman style, this would be number one because of its pedagogical elegance and adaptability. The Sticky Notes Bookmark combines the convenience of a built-in schedule with sticky notes for the purpose of teaching students how to annotate texts when prompted by various critical perspectives. Coming up with it took me only about, oh, I'd say a decade.

Many years ago, the National Council of Teachers of English created a reproducible timetable bookmark to help students complete independent reading assignments in a timely manner. I've never forgotten how much my students loved the practicality of the bookmark because the reading schedule was always handy, right inside their book. A few years later, I discovered that sticky notes were another convenient tool for teaching an equally important skill—annotating texts that belong to the book room. When I was an undergraduate English major, annotations were essential in creating a record of my reading, but as an English teacher, I quickly realized students must show respect for future readers who wouldn't look kindly on already marked-on texts. I couldn't ask my students to write in school books, but when sticky notes came along, I found a wonderful alternative. Students were able to temporarily annotate their books and simply remove the sticky notes when it came time to return the texts to the book room.

Several years later, at my daughter's junior high, I was assisting with lunchtime book clubs made up of self-selected students participating only for extra credit and their own enjoyment. Emily Richards Moyer, the teacher organizing the project, wanted to encourage outside reading, open-ended response, and authentic book club discussion. Students negotiated a reasonable reading schedule, but they needed personal reminders since they wouldn't be getting these daily in class. The timetable bookmark immediately came to mind since the book club was mostly social in nature, and students weren't interested in piling lengthy journal responses on top of their homework. When I mentioned the sticky notes, the students agreed that these would help prompt discussion topics for book club without interrupting momentum in their reading. "But when are sticky notes called for?" students wanted to know.

Answering this question led to the invention of the Sticky Notes Bookmark. In Appendix C I've included five variations of the Sticky Notes Bookmark. When you compare the bookmarks at a glance, though, you'll see their common features. Each one has three columns, and in the first, students record their reading schedule. The second column details instructions for using the bookmark in conjunction with sticky notes. The third column provides a list of prompts to guide students' use of the sticky notes according to various critical perspectives.

The prompts on the textual approach bookmark guided Katrina, a student in Rebecca Fox's class, when she was reading *In the Time of the Butterflies*, by Isabel Allende. On her sticky notes, Katrina marked examples of literary techniques (e.g., foreshadowing, flashback, irony, etc.), asked questions, and made miscellaneous observations like the following:

- Weird

- I get it!

- How Mate has changed from this → to this → [pointing from one area of the text to another]

- Struck me. After all he went through, he still fought.

- Wow! Telling of death

- Almost even worse! She in a way was killed with her sisters.

The bookmarks work so well, I've used them with readers in fifth grade through college. Again, students appreciate seeing a reminder of the reading schedule—and now, the response prompts as well—every time they mark their place in the book. The sticky notes are a big hit, too. Besides the fact that they come in cool colors, students like them because they don't slow down their reading. Sticky notes also work better than a highlighter since they provide enough room for a brief note to self, helping students remember later why they marked a particular point in the text. In book clubs, sticky notes are also great reminders of topics students want to bring up in book club discussions, especially because they ground discussion right back in the text, as you can see from Katrina's examples.

**STICKY NOTES AND THE APPLICATION OF LITERARY THEORIES** Before moving on, I want to say more about how the prompts on the bookmark can provide embedded instruction in the application of various critical perspectives as well. As you'll see when you look at the variations of the bookmark in Appendix C, you can easily adjust the prompts so that they align with the critical perspectives you are teaching at the time. I designed the first bookmark for eighth graders. The prompts on this bookmark are informed mostly by reader response theory (e.g., Rosenblatt 1978). The remaining bookmarks are meant for high school students and are informed by four critical perspectives—textual, social, topical, and cultural (Beach and Marshall 1991). This framework provides a generalized, but accessible entry into literary theory, which even mature readers can often find daunting.

Because readers bring different kinds of knowledge to their reading experiences, the four perspectives are "meant to serve . . . as a heuristic, as an overlapping category system that may allow teachers to think about their teaching, and students to think about their response" (Beach and Marshall 1991, 247). Briefly, the *textual* approach focuses on structural concerns, teaching students methods of close reading. The *social* approach prompts emotional and experiential connections to texts and other readers, while the *topical* approach draws on outside knowledge from different academic fields, such as history, science, and music, to inform readers' understanding of relevant topics in the text. Finally, the *cultural* approach examines the influence of larger social and cultural forces, such as race, gender, and class, on the text as well as the reader.

While these four types of knowledge overlap, I have found it useful at the beginning of my literature courses to apply each individually to four texts in turn, as recommended when teaching adolescent readers literary theory (Appleman 2000; Moore 1997; Soter 1999). Yes, this progression is artificial, but it is purposely so, and, most importantly, it is *only temporary*. I'm careful to point out to students that real readers just don't read this way, first noting the plot structure of a text before connecting to it emotionally, for instance.

My purpose for this isolation is to help them understand how the critical perspectives we use when viewing texts are instrumental in shaping our eventual interpretations. Students just get it better when we apply one approach at a time, but before moving on to the next approach, I also ask them to discuss the benefits and limitations they observe when applying a given perspective. Students also reflect on their degree of comfort, or lack thereof, with the approach at hand and consider why this may be the case. Combined with this sort of reflection, the experience of working through all four perspectives provides students with a range of critical tools to help them interpret the subsequent texts they will read in the course. They also should be more aware of when they are privileging certain perspectives and why.

Using the Sticky Notes Bookmarks, the most natural progression I've found through the perspectives is to start with the textual and then move to the social, the topical, and the cultural, in that order. Proceeding in this fashion has the advantage of starting with the particular reader and moving outward toward progressively broader concerns. Why begin with the textual perspective? In short, because students find it familiar territory. If you sense strains of New Criticism theory (e.g., Richards 1929) in the textual approach, you aren't mistaken. Even if New Criticism has left a bad taste in your mouth, however, I encourage you to start here because subsequent literary theories are built on the assumption that readers are able to read texts closely. In addition, as you'll see on the textual Sticky Notes Bookmark, a focus on literary elements doesn't necessarily demand that readers arrive at a single privileged interpretation of a text (read, one right answer). Textual prompts can still be open-ended.

The bookmarks themselves provide a condensed, but detailed overview of Beach and Marshall's (1991) framework, but if you find you need to bone up on your literary theory, Appleman (2000), Moore (1997), and Soter (1999) provide accessible reviews in reference to oft-taught texts in secondary classrooms. *Falling into Theory*, edited by David Richter (2000), is another useful resource, as is the Case Studies in Contemporary Criticism series published by Bedford Books. This series accompanies full-length texts like *The Awakening* and *The Scarlet Letter* with analytical essays written from various critical perspectives.

In the previous discussion, I've taken it for granted that you think teaching a range of critical perspectives is a good idea, but I realize that this may not be the case. You may think your students aren't developmentally ready for such heady stuff, that learning to be critical can rob students of their reading pleasure, or that teaching theory is too political.

On the first count, remember that especially in book clubs, the focus is less on theory per se and more on helping your students consider how critical perspectives shape the questions readers ask of literary texts and the interpretations that result. That's why I've used Beach and Marshall's (1991) framework to introduce students to a limited number of perspectives via the sticky notes bookmarks. Furthermore, the age of your students should help you determine how detailed to be in explaining the theoretical principles behind the response tools you're asking them to use. Thoreau's advice to make things as simple as possible, but not simpler, definitely applies here.

In other words, I've gone into far more detail about literary theories with college students than I have with sixth graders. It's also helped me to remember that regardless of what theoretical lenses readers choose, they need the tools of close reading to employ them. Finally, I remind myself that literary theory is primarily a metacognitive concern—for me, in terms of instructional design, and for my students, in terms of reflection on their thinking and discussion. In other words, while theory can shape book club discussion, it generally isn't the object of it.

When reading Linda Christensen's *Reading, Writing, and Rising Up* (2000), my college students objected to her insistence that high school readers need to analyze stereotypes in children's cartoons, movies, and literature. My students felt that this approach would destroy adolescent readers' innocence by complicating the pleasure young viewers and readers typically feel when consuming such texts. Christensen argues convincingly, however, that if adolescents are to "wrestle with the social text of novels, news, or history books, they need the tools to critique media that encourage or legitimate social inequality" (41). Critical theories comprise these tools.

Finally, you might reason that teaching theory is too political, that it's a parent's job to teach kids what to think, not yours. The more interesting question, however, is Who teaches kids *how* to think? I can't think of a politician who doesn't laud the value of critical thinking in one breath and then criticize schools in the next for not teaching kids how to do it. I'd say it's virtually impossible to separate the *what* from the *how*, and that does mean there are political repercussions to teaching a multiplicity of theoretical perspectives. But because teaching is always a political act (Freire 1995), teaching kids just one interpretation is at least as political as allowing for multiple interpretations (Edelsky 1992, 1994; Hynds 1997). There are no algorithms for literary analysis, and the lens through which the reader views the text inevitably colors the final (can there ever really be a final?) interpretation (Appleman 2000).

If you've decided to try book clubs, you've already decided to grant kids the freedom to make choices in your classroom. By choosing books, they're in effect negotiating the literature curriculum with you. Shouldn't this freedom also extend to the perspectives they use to read the books they've chosen? If so, it's not only important to provide students with a box full of response tools but also crucial to be clear—first to yourself and eventually to them—that response tools inevitably imply theoretical perspectives. Close reading strategies are an important place to start, but let's not be idiocentric when it's such a big, beautiful theoretical world out there.

## Before Moving On

Let's recap what you've done so far. A week or so before the first book club session, you've given your *book talks* and students have submitted their top three *choices*. Based on these choices and your instincts about social dynamics, you've *organized students* into book clubs and announced who will be reading what. Students have made a *reading schedule* and met in their book club to devise a set of *book club norms*. You've also selected a *response tool* students will use to record their reactions to the text and stimulate exploratory discussion.

The only task that remains is to *teach students how to use the response tool*. Sometimes a brief explanation and an example of the tool will suffice. Other times, especially early in the year, you may need to provide more scaffolding, like that I describe in Chapter 2 in reference to reading logs. Once you're confident that students understand the reading schedule, how book clubs will run, and how to use the response tool, they're ready to start reading. A week later, book clubs can begin.

## On the First Day: Preparing for Discussion, Moving Furniture, and Keeping Track

Before students move into book clubs the first day, I ask them to make some decisions about the responses they'd like to share. This routine will become old hat soon enough, but in the beginning, students need explicit instructions on how to use their individual responses to fuel their discussion. Here's what I ask them to do:

1. Take a few minutes to read back over your response.

2. In the margins of your paper, use a star to mark three to four points you've made that you'd like to share with your book club. These may be insights you've reached, passages you want to point out, questions you want to ask, or evaluations you want to make.

3. Next, rank each item, putting a 1 by the item you most want to discuss, a 2 by the next most important item, and so on. In the event that you run out of time, this will ensure that you get to discuss your most important ideas.

4. Use these items to fuel your book club discussion. Remember that you want this to be a conversation, so you don't necessarily need to go around the circle one at a time (but you can if this works for your group!). Just be sure that everyone has equal airtime and that you're honoring your own ground rules.

5. Be sure to record the most important point made by each book club member on the Book Club Discussion Record.

6. Any questions?

I'll talk more about the Book Club Discussion Record in a moment, but the next step is making sure students know, literally, what a book club looks like. The first time we asked kids to move into book clubs in Rebecca Fox's classroom, I overheard a kid mutter, "An awful lot of desk moving goes on in here," as he pushed his desk into a tight circle with his other book club members. He was right. If you've taught very long, you know that helping kids get down to the business of literacy learning often involves moving chairs out of neat rows. Can you even imagine a book club functioning well in such a traditional setup? Probably not, but kids need more reminding than you might think.

Toward the beginning of the year, I actually make this a point of discussion in a minilesson I call "Furniture Moving 101." I ask students to think about how spaces are configured in different settings such as churches, gymnasiums, theatres, doctors' offices, science labs, and classrooms. Quickly, they are able to see how the physical arrangements of spaces suggest mindsets that channel particular modes of interaction. Then I explain that we will rearrange the furniture often, depending on the task at hand. In book clubs, the circle is the shape of choice because it's important that everyone is able to make eye contact with and hear what other members of the group are saying. I actually pull chairs into a tight circle to demonstrate. Once students know how to rearrange the furniture and have individually ranked their discussion topics, they are ready to start talking.

Effective student-led discussion is characterized by the following essential features of small groups (Alvermann et al. 1996):

◈ student-selected topics that provide opportunities for interpretation, expression of varied opinions, and clarification of ideas

◈ open-ended tasks that require group collaboration, as opposed to division of labor among individuals

◈ clear guidelines for how to hold a focused and respectful discussion in which all members participate

Book clubs clearly meet the first two criteria because students have chosen their books and have used open-ended response tools to determine what they'd like to discuss. Having set their own goals and ground rules, students are also well on their way to the third criterion. The Book Club Discussion Record I mentioned in Chapter 3 (also see Appendix B–2) can help seal the deal. An example completed by Rebecca's students (see Figure 5.3) shows how the discussion record provides space for discussion highlights as well as response to one real question you'll want to ask each time.

If you've ever taken a literature class that was organized around class discussion rather than the traditional lecture, you know how enlightening the experience can be. You also may have come to the end of the class with little more than warm memories of the discussion that occurred because it can be difficult to record all the great ideas that get kicked around and verbally participate at the same time. The discussion record is useful in this regard for a couple of reasons.

First, it helps students keep track of the highlights of their conversations, which tend to be characterized by a free-flowing quality if all is going well. Rotating the role of recorder means that no student has to take the backseat for more than one session, and even then he or she can still participate to some extent since only the highlights are to be recorded. Second, the discussion record lends some structure, though not rigid by any means, to students' conversations and implies equitable participation. They know that in the allotted time—usually twenty to thirty minutes, depending on the age and discussion experience of the students—they need to make a record of *everyone's* contribution and consider the teacher question listed at the bottom of the discussion record as well. Even though you can't be everywhere at one time as you're browsing around the room, the teacher question allows you to be subtly present in every book club, especially since students know you'll be collecting and reviewing discussion records after each book club session. It also allows you to have some instructional influence in every session and provides a common thread among book clubs.

In addition to collecting discussion records, you also need to keep track of students' individual responses. Students will need these at the end of the book club cycle as they are working on final projects, and collecting their responses after each session allows you to pace your grading and see how individual students are coming along. The organizational method that works best for me is to staple students' individual responses to the back of their group's discussion record after each book club. If I'm making written comments, I try to do so before the next book club meeting. That way I can distribute the papers so that students can take a quick look before they begin that day's discussion. Then I take the responses back up, staple each group's packet together, and file them together under "Book Club

Date: <u>10/18</u> Book Title: <u>*In the Time of the Butterflies*</u> Group Name: <u>Man-Eating Flutterbys</u>

Group Discussion Leader: <u>Callie</u>          Scribe: <u>Madison</u>

(Please choose a different person for each session) (Please choose a different person for each session.)

Other Group Members Present: <u>Kayla, Katrina, Julie, Selena</u>

Group members absent: <u>*NONE!*</u>

**Main Ideas Generated from Real Books Letters:** Please write a one-sentence summary of the most significant ideas or questions contributed by each book club member. Write the group member's name beside her/his idea or question.

1. Katrina: Patria is moved to join cause with the death of the boy.

2. Madison: El Jefe is portrayed as a sexual predator.

3. Kayla: Maria Teresa is *muy gulible!* Rather endearing.

4. Callie: Saw foreshadowing when she left her purse at the party.

5. Selena: Maria Teresa—foreshadowing violent actions: "I would never take up a gun to stop being mean." "My best friends are men who work"—description of El Jefe.

6. Julie: Patria related her personality, which is expressed in domestication, to the Revolution.

**Today's Question(s):**

1. *The word* conflict *comes from Latin and literally means "to strike together." Identify the forces that are striking against one another in your protagonist's life at this point and discuss whether these forces are internal, external, or both.*

2. *If your protagonist were to open a fortune cookie at this point in the book, what might he/she find? Write a one-sentence fortune predicting the outcome of one of these conflicts for your character and be prepared to explain it to the rest of the class.*

**Your Conclusions:**

1. We saw both—External force of El Jefe and internal forces of deciding stance on Revolution

2. Fortune for Minerva: "You will sacrifice everything for a good cause. LUCKY NUMBER 457-1322-4824."

FIG. 5.3. *Sample Book Club Discussion Record*

Discussion 1," "Book Club Discussion 2," and so on, until the end of the book club cycle when students begin their final projects.

So what else should you be doing during book clubs? Browsing, observing, troubleshooting if necessary. And *briefly* dropping in if you can do so without dominating the discussion or turning all eyes toward you. Just remember that no matter how well meaning you may be, your teacherly presence will inevitably influence students' interaction. Also, you'll want to get around to every group, so don't stay for long.

As the time you've allotted for book clubs comes to a close, you may also want to bring students back together as a whole class to report out on the common question listed at the bottom of the discussion record. Whether you do this or not will probably depend on how much time is left in the class period, what the question is, and whether you think hearing other students' responses to it might provide another teaching opportunity. This can also be a time for students to reflect generally on their book club participation and for you to share what you've observed about their learning during their discussions.

In the next chapter on assessment, I share a teacher-research tool for helping you mindfully collect these observations. I also describe other strategies for determining how students are doing along the way and at the end of the line as well.

# Assessing, Evaluating, and Grading Students' Book Club Performances

As students engage in exploratory discussion and composition during book clubs, you'll have many opportunities along the way to assess and evaluate their book club performance. While Chapter 5 focused on the ongoing texts and tasks that will allow you to do so *during* book club, this chapter focuses primarily on the texts and tasks students will complete *after* finishing the book. These culminating texts and tasks look very different from the traditional tests I administered at the beginning of my career.

When I began teaching English in 1987, I also coached drama, an experience that changed my teaching right away and influenced the way I assessed my students' learning a few years later. I knew firsthand that memorizing lines, inferring a character's motivations, blocking scenes, and connecting with others on stage were extraordinary ways of exploring texts from the inside out. Consequently, the activities in my English classes reflected the hands-on, yet deeply analytical, nature of drama classes.

A few years later, my experiential rationale that students learn through creative and purposeful activity—talking, writing, moving, and making things connected to the concepts and texts at hand in our classroom—found a theoretical framework in the multiple intelligences theory of Howard Gardner (1983, 1993). I began to think about how my own beliefs and Gardner's theories ought to be reflected in the *assessment* of my students' work as well. While my students learned about literature by creating visual interpretations, generating real questions and discussing them in small groups, dramatizing scenes, and adapting texts into children's books, I still considered the crowning achievement of their learning to be a pen-and-paper test. The disconnect was so jarring, I began to seriously ask myself, "How well do my methods of assessment and evaluation at the end connect with students' methods of learning along the way?"

Although I was no longer coaching drama by then, reflecting on the ways I had assessed my student actors was instructive for me. Planning backward from our performance date, I had designed a rehearsal schedule I felt would prepare students for the play. At the first rehearsal, I clarified roles and expectations for the entire cast and crew. Then we spent the first few rehearsals sitting in a circle and reading through the script, analyzing and discussing characters' motivations and the social dynamics of the play. Actors experimented with different ways of delivering their lines, and then we got the play on its feet, blocking the action and determining stage business and placement of props.

All the while, I carefully observed students' performances in practice and provided on-the-spot direction accordingly. My rehearsal notes also informed my planning for the next day's rehearsal, helping me figure out what adjustments I'd need to make to warm-ups and whether or not I needed to engage the cast in a drama exercise, fine-tune a scene, or confer with an individual actor. This *ongoing assessment* of students' performances during rehearsals helped me prepare them adequately for the performance of the entire play, or the *culminating text* (Smagorinsky 2002) they produced, if you will. My finest hope, however, was that my students' involvement in the production would help them develop an *enduring involvement* of some kind in theatre, whether they were performing on stage or sitting in the audience.

In other words, when I taught drama, my methods of assessment and evaluation clearly connected with students' methods of learning along the way. The celebration of their accomplishments at the cast party and their willingness a few weeks later to audition for yet another production suggested that they were eager to continue developing as performers. Although I knew my English students would never throw a party at the end of a literature unit, I did want my teaching and assessment methods to be more closely aligned. And I did want my students to become "successful readers" in the sense that Bud Hunt describes them: "students who, because of their successes with one book, will likely approach a second book, and a third. . . . [A]fter my class is over, they just might keep reading" (Hunt and Hunt 2004, 98). This doesn't mean I quit giving essay tests entirely, because I knew students still would see them beyond the classroom. However, pen-and-paper assignments were no longer the exclusive form of assessment.

And this was especially true for book clubs. I reasoned that since book clubs are geared toward students' performances as readers, thinkers, and composers, my principles for assessment and evaluation ought to parallel those from my drama-teaching days. As a result, the following principles still guide my methods of book club assessment:

- The ongoing and culminating assessment of students' literacy development during book clubs ought to be performance based.

- Students' ongoing tasks during book club should prepare them to produce the culminating assessments I have in mind for them *after* they finish their books.

- The culminating assessment should provide an "occasion for new learning" (Smagorinsky 2002, 72) based on students' preceding book club experiences.

- If assessment is to extend students' learning (i.e., allow them to construct and explore, rather than merely report, what they're learning), then both ongoing tasks and culminating assessments should provide students with creative and open-ended opportunities for literary interpretation and personal reflection.

- Ideally, assessment should be an opportunity rather than an obligation, prompting in students a "continuing impulse to learn" (Oldfather 1993).

These principles are also informed by position statements that describe what adolescent readers deserve in literacy assessment published by the International Reading Association (2000), the National Council of Teachers of English (NCTE Commission on Reading 2004a, 2004b), and the National Middle Schools Association (IRA and NMSA 2002). In particular, the NCTE Commission on Reading argues that reading assessment should be in situ, that is, it should focus on thinking strategies students use in the midst of literacy acts rather than on the recall of isolated facts in the text after reading (2004a). Consequently, assessment of readers must not be limited to standardized measures and traditional tests but should include a range of evidence like classroom observations, writing samples, and multimodal responses beyond writing, such as art, drama, storytelling, and music. Finally, effective classroom assessments should be based on standards and performance, offer clear and usable feedback, and involve students in the evaluation process, contends the position statement published by the Commission on Adolescent Literacy of the International

Reading Association (Moore et al. 1999). Taken together, these arguments emphasize that although giving a published, multiple-choice test about a book may seem efficient and properly objective, if we really want to assess readers effectively, we must focus on doing what's best for kids as opposed to what's easiest for us.

You might have guessed by now that my favorite tasks and texts for students to complete at the end of book club do not resemble the traditional test. Rather, they are rooted in the principles and recommendations I've outlined earlier in that they are performance based, in situ, multimodal, guided by standards (NCTE and IRA 1996), and connected to prior instruction. But before moving on to my favorite tools for assessment and evaluation, I need to clarify some terminology.

## Some Important Terminological Distinctions

Though the terms *assessment*, *evaluation*, and *grading* are often used interchangeably, Kathleen and James Strickland (1998) distinguish between them in useful ways. *Assessment* refers to "a collection of data, information that enlightens the teacher and the learner, information that drives instruction" (19). *Evaluation*, on the other hand, is the "product of assessment" (20). It refers to the conclusions teachers draw about their students' progress based on their analysis of the data they've collected. Scoring guides, or rubrics, are useful evaluation tools because they delineate the criteria teachers will use to analyze the data they've collected and the quality indicators they will use to inform their *grading*, the "assignment of a numerical score, letter, or percentage to a product" (21). To sum up, assessment is the data-gathering stage, evaluation is the data-analysis stage, and grading is the assigning of a score and the reporting of the value we place upon the data we've analyzed.

I also want to distinguish between *ongoing* and *culminating* tasks and texts students produce throughout the book club process. The tasks you ask students to perform *during* book club (e.g., reading, annotating, and responding to their books, talking about them in exploratory ways, keeping track of their discussions, etc.) and the texts you ask them to produce as a result (e.g., reading logs, sticky notes, discussion records, etc.) are the *ongoing* sources of data you collect to evaluate students' book club performances. In my Top Ten Toolbox from Chapter 5, I've already discussed these *ongoing tasks and texts* in detail, but in the next section, I provide methods for assessment, evaluation, and grading. The bulk of this chapter, however, is devoted to another toolbox, this time of *culminating texts*, along with resources for evaluation and grading. Students produce these texts *after* they've finished their book club books as a way of synthesizing what they've learned.

## A Couple of Resources for Assessing and Evaluating Ongoing Tasks and Texts

At the end of Chapter 5, I explained that one of your jobs during actual book clubs is observing students' interactions, and I promised you a method of keeping track of your observations. The Field Notes Journal is it (see Appendix B–3). It's actually a combination of two data collection methods—recording field notes and journaling—that teacher researchers often use to help them devote systematic attention to the questions that arise during teaching.

The Field Notes Journal is organized like a typical double-entry journal. In the left-hand column, you record your *observations* of what actually happened during the book club session; the right-hand column is for your *reflections* on these events. The "To Think About" section at the bottom of the page is a handy place to summarize your impressions and note anything you want to think about further, especially before the next book club session. To begin keeping a Field Notes Journal, simply photocopy the master, punch holes in the side of it, and collect your entries in a loose-leaf notebook. During book clubs, I like to keep several copies on a clipboard so I can take notes as I browse around the room. If you prefer, though, you can also just hand copy the form into a regular spiral or hardcover journal.

Sometimes I go into a book club session with a question already in mind. Then I gear my observations and reflections toward exploring possible answers. Just as often, however, especially at the beginning of the year or at the start of a book club cycle, I go in without a specific question and trust that something interesting will occur. Because my students know I am a teacher-researcher, they are used to seeing the Field Notes Journal in my hand. They know that I'm using it as a tool for understanding how they're learning, and as I described in Chapter 3, they are usually eager to respond further to the questions and hunches that arise there. These brief discussions often occur after a book club session in the last few minutes of class, and they usually begin with my comment "I noticed something interesting during book club today. Could you help me understand what was happening?"

Just as I need ongoing feedback of this sort to guide my teaching, my students need feedback to the ongoing texts they're producing. To manage the paper load, I typically use a checkpoint system, sometimes combined with brief readerly comments, to respond to the exploratory writing students produce during book club. A handout I give to students describes this system (see Appendix C–15), which I adapted from Tom Romano's *Writing with Passion* (1995). I also employ scoring guides for the kinds of culminating texts I ask students to produce at the conclusion of a book club cycle. But first, to the texts themselves.

## My Favorite Culminating Texts

Rather than describe every single culminating text I've ever developed for book clubs, I present four of my favorites in the Final Four Toolbox chart (see Figure 6.1), which use Beach and Marshall's (1991) critical perspectives. Each of these projects allows students to keep learning by requiring them to synthesize what they've learned throughout the book club sessions, make interpretive claims about their books, and justify them with evidence and analysis. Aside from the fact that students seem to enjoy producing them a great deal, the projects thus help students learn to "'do English' instead of just regurgitating facts" (Strickland and Strickland 1998, 69). Part of students' enjoyment likely stems from the projects' multimodal approach to literary interpretation, for each combines exploratory talk, writing, visualization, and presentation. Activities that make reading visible are sorely needed in schools because they help students learn from and about each other's reading processes, as Smith and Wilhelm (2002) point out. These projects allow students (and you) to literally "see what they mean."

When I studied small groups of my high school students as they produced Body Biographies, a visual autobiography I adapted into a character analysis assignment (Underwood 1987), I discovered that they drew on their personal experiences, prior texts, and literary knowledge to make life-size visual interpretations of characters from *Hamlet* (Smagorinsky and O'Donnell-Allen 1998b). In their collaborative analysis of a character, students used exploratory talk to develop their interpretation on four planes:

| Strategy | Featured Perspective | What It Is | When to Use It |
|---|---|---|---|
| Life Map | Textual | A mural visualizing the most significant events in the life of the book | Assign Life Maps when you want students to analyze the structural elements of their book club book. |
| Body Biography | Social | A life-size visual and written portrait illustrating several aspects of a character's life | Assign Body Biographies when you want students to define their social relationship with their book club book by evaluating (1.) the writer's motives for telling the story, (2.) the sources of characters' behaviors and relationships, and (3.) the sources of readers' own responses. |
| Censorship Scenario | Topical | A scenario in which students research various aspects of a topic (e.g., censorship) central to their book and dramatize roles in relation to it | Assign scenarios like this one when you want students to apply their background knowledge of different fields or topics (e.g., censorship) to their understanding of their book club book. This approach encourages an intertextual perspective. |
| Cultural Studies Project | Cultural | A presentation analyzing an institution or issue from contemporary culture in relation to the same institution or issue as it is represented in the book | Assign projects like this one when you want students to examine how the expectations, values, and conventions of different institutional or cultural forces shape their book club book as well as their responses to and understanding of the book. |

FIG. 6.1. *Final Four Toolbox*

1. *Literal Interpretation.* Students discussed events, names, and details from the play as they considered "What happened?"

2. *Developing Interpretation.* They made inferences about the text, explored themes, and made claims about the character's attitudes and motivations as they considered "What does it mean?"

3. *Symbolic Interpretation.* They determined how to use art and words to display their interpretive claims as they considered "How can we represent this meaning?"

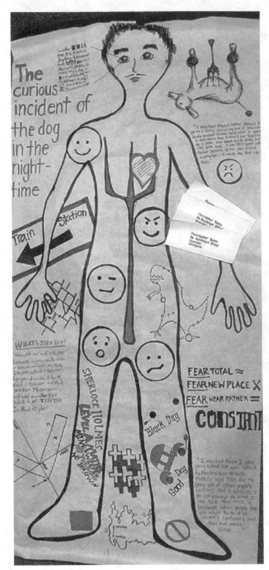

FIG. 6.2. *Body Biography for* The Curious Incident of the Dog in Night-Time

**4.** *Reflection.* They verbally defended their final product during the presentation of their Body Biography as they considered "How can we defend our conclusions?"

Instead of moving sequentially, students moved back and forth among these planes, sometimes clarifying a plot detail, for instance, as they sketched a symbol representing a significant event.

What was most remarkable was how students constructed new meaning at every stage of production in their Body Biographies, arriving at new insight about their characters even as they were making their final presentations to the class. This study also demonstrated how multimodal projects like this can engage students in sophisticated literary thinking, even about texts as complex as Shakespeare's. In addition to helping students engage with written texts in the same way they do with multimedia ones, culminating texts like the ones I describe here "foreground the fact that reading is an active and transactional meaning-making pursuit that involves them, their backgrounds, their interests, their concerns, and their opinions" (Smith and Wilhelm 2002, 132). Rebecca Fox's students created the sample Body Biography I've included here (see Figure 6.2).

The Final Four Toolbox chart (Figure 6.1) allows you to see all four culminating texts at a glance. In it, I briefly describe the assignment, identify the critical perspective it is meant to feature, and recommend when to use it.

In Appendix D, you'll find detailed assignment sheets for each culminating text accompanied by scoring guides. By simply changing the prompts on the assignment sheets, you'll find that these culminating texts are remarkably adaptable to the instructional concepts you want to emphasize. The number of variations is limited only by your imagination.

# A Final Word

In *Walk the Line*, the movie on Johnny Cash's life, there's this wonderful moment when Cash and his buddies are auditioning in a recording studio. In the middle of a gospel standard, the record producer stops them and says he can't sell what they're singing. When Cash won't leave, the producer challenges him to deliver a song someone can believe in, the tune he'd choose in the gutter if he knew he had only one song left to sing. Cash swallows hard and digs deep into an original. That night, he and the Tennessee Two go on to make the record that launches their career.

The most important thing we can do as teachers is to figure out what constitutes our equivalent of the song that we believe in.

Before I close, I want you to think back to the earliest books in your memory. Mine are books my mother read to me, and I can still see them clearly. Beatrix Potter's delicate watercolors of Peter Rabbit devouring carrots from Mr. MacGregor's garden. The checkerboard pattern framing Mother Goose, looking rather witchy in her striped stockings and black pointy hat.

I met these books on my mother's lap, leaning back, listening close to the book propped up in front of me. She would read a while and then stop for my questions. We would talk about why Peter was naughty but also a little brave and marvel at all the children spilling out of the old woman's shoe. It was my first book club, and I've been caught ever since in that triangle of literature, love, and lamplight.

I also want to catch my students there and yours, too, choosing books they want to read and talking them over with people they care about. Somehow, some little way, I hope this book will help you do it. If it does, I've sung the song that I believe in.

# Appendix A

*Resources for Text Selection*

## CONTENTS

## A-1 Text Selection Planning Guide

| | Assessments | Standards | My Instructional Goals | Students' Preferences and Needs |
|---|---|---|---|---|
| **Questions I Need to Consider** | What major assessments will students encounter at the end of book club?<br><br>At the end of my course? | What standards should/could I address through book clubs? | What do I want students to get out of book clubs?<br><br>How should the texts be linked together (e.g., by theme, genre, historical period, common focus or content, author, literary style, etc.)? | What content and text features will my students consider engaging?<br><br>What immediate student needs do I need to consider? |
| **My Answers** | | | | |
| **Resulting Criteria** | | | | |
| **Texts That Come to Mind** | | | | |
| **Methods of Securing Books** | • Book room<br>• Student purchase with bookstore discount<br>• Department, school, or district textbook monies<br>• Beg and borrow (school and local libraries)<br>• Grants or partnerships (university, professional organizations, PTO)<br>• Donations (local businesses, community foundations, etc.)<br>• Other _____ | | | |

# A–2 Book Club Text Clusters

A *text cluster* is a set of related texts to use in a single book club cycle. To help you start thinking about possibilities for organizing books, I've recommended four text clusters per grade level (six through twelve)—two organized by theme and one each by genre and author. None of the clusters is meant to be hard-and-fast. I suspect you'll want to mix and match texts from surrounding grade levels, substitute your own selections, and augment these lists based on books available at your school. I've listed three to five titles in each category, along with authors' names. When I've listed a smaller number of titles, usually in the category of author study, my assumption is that more than one book club will be reading the same book.

My goal was to choose a blend of classic and contemporary titles by diverse authors writing for a range of reading levels. To compile the list, I relied on my own teaching and book club experiences, followed recommendations made by Colorado State University Writing Project teachers and adolescent readers, and reviewed various honor lists and Don Gallo's *English Journal* column "Bold Books for Innovative Teaching."

## Sixth Grade

### THEME: FINDING MY PLACE
*Because of Winn Dixie*—Kate DiCamillo
*Call Me María*—Judith Ortiz Cofer
*Dovey Coe*—Frances O'Roark Dowell
*Maniac Magee*—Jerry Spinelli
*When Zachary Beaver Came to Town*—Kimberly Willis Holt

### THEME: WORLDS APART
*Bridge to Terabithia*—Katherine Paterson
*A Door Near Here*—Heather Quarles
*The Lion, the Witch, and the Wardrobe*—C. S. Lewis
*Tuck Everlasting*—Natalie Babbitt
*A Wrinkle in Time*—Madeline L'Engle

### AUTHOR STUDY: GARY PAULSEN
*Harris and Me*
*Hatchet*

*My Life in Dog Years*
*Nightjohn*
*Sarny, A Life Remembered*

**GENRE STUDY: HISTORICAL FICTION**
*Fever, 1793*—Laurie Halse Anderson
*Milkweed*—Jerry Spinelli
*My Brother Sam Is Dead*—James L. and Christopher Collier
*Roll of Thunder, Hear My Cry*—Mildred Taylor
*Witness*—Karen Hesse

## Seventh Grade

**THEME: HOLDING ON AND LETTING GO**
*Bird*—Angela Johnson
*A Fast and Brutal Wing*—Kathleen Jeffrie Johnson
*The Gravedigger's Cottage*—Christopher Lynch
*Out of the Dust*—Karen Hesse
*The Schwa Was Here*—Neal Shusterman

**THEME: TIES THAT BIND**
*Al Capone Does My Shirts*—Gennifer Coldenko
*Holes*—Louis Sachar
*Silent to the Bone*—E. L. Konigsburg
*The True Confessions of Charlotte Doyle*—Avi
*The Young Man and the Sea*—Rodman Philbrick

**AUTHOR STUDY: SHARON CREECH**
*Bloomability*
*Chasing Redbird*
*Walk Two Moons*
*The Wanderer*

**GENRE STUDY: SUPERNATURAL TALES**
*The Ghost in the Tokaido Inn*—Dorothy and Thomas Hoobler
*The Haunting*—Joan Lowery Nixon
*Kit's Wilderness*—David Almond
*The Moonlight Man*—Betty Ren Wright
*Skellig*—David Almond

## Eighth Grade

**THEME: STANDING OUT, BLENDING IN**

*Aquamarine*—Alice Hoffman
*Freak the Mighty*—Rodman Philbrick
*Gingerbread*—Rachel Cohn
*Kokopelli's Flute*—Will Hobbs
*Stargirl*—Jerry Spinelli

**THEME: ON MY OWN**

*An Acquaintance with Darkness*—Ann Rinaldi
*The Diary of Anne Frank*
*Hoot*—Carl Hiaasen
*Kissing the Rain*—Kevin Brooks
*Memoirs of a Bookbat*—Kathryn Lasky

**AUTHOR STUDY: LOIS LOWRY**

*Gathering Blue*
*The Giver*
*The Messenger*
*The Silent Boy*

**GENRE STUDY: FANTASY**

*City of the Beasts*—Isabel Allende
*Eragon*—Christopher Paolini
*The Golden Compass*—Phillip Pullman
*The Hobbit*—J. R. R. Tolkien
*The Thief Lord*—Cornelia Funke

## Ninth Grade

**THEME: COMING OF AGE**

*Choosing Up Sides*—John H. Ritter
*The River Between Us*—Richard Peck
*A Separate Peace*—John Knowles
*A Step from Heaven*—An Na
*To Kill a Mockingbird*—Harper Lee

**THEME: OUTCASTS**

*Godless*—Pete Hautman

*The Outsiders*—S. E. Hinton

*Romiette and Julio*—Sharon M. Draper

*Scribbler of Dreams*—Mary E. Pearson

*Speak*—Laurie Halse Anderson

**AUTHOR STUDY: WALTER DEAN MYERS**

*Autobiography of My Dead Brother*

*Bad Boy*

*Fallen Angels*

*Monster*

*Slam*

**GENRE STUDY: SHORT STORY**

*145th Street*—Walter Dean Myers

*Athletic Shorts*—Chris Crutcher

collected short stories—Edgar Allan Poe

*Night Shift*—Stephen King

*What a Song Can Do*—Jennifer Armstrong (editor)

## Tenth Grade

**THEME: STANDING OUT AND BLENDING IN**

*The Chocolate War*—Robert Cormier

*The Outsiders*—S. E. Hinton

*Saving Francesca*—Melina Marchetta

*Son of the Mob*—Gordon Korman

*Speak*—Laurie Halse Anderson

**THEME: SURVIVAL**

*All Quiet on the Western Front*—Erich Maria Remarque

*The First Part Last*—Angela Johnson

*How I Live Now*—Meg Rosoff

*Into Thin Air*—Jon Krakauer

*Tree Girl*—Ben Mikaelson

**AUTHOR STUDY: ART SPIEGELMAN**

*In the Shadow of No Towers*

*Maus 1*
*Maus 2*

**GENRE STUDY: MYSTERY**

*The Body of Christopher Creed*—Carol Plum-Ucci
*The Client*—John Grisham
*A Great and Terrible Beauty*—Libba Bray
*Murder on the Orient Express*—Agatha Christie
*A Northern Light*—Jennifer Donnelly

## Eleventh Grade

**THEME: SECRETS AND LIES**

*In the Time of the Butterflies*—Julia Alvarez
*Montana, 1948*—Larry Watson
*My Heartbeat*—Garret Freymann-Weyr
*The Secret Diary of Adrian Mole, Age 13¾*—Sue Townsend
*What Girls Learn*—Karin Cook

**THEME: GENDER ROLES**

*The Awakening*—Kate Chopin
*Bless Me, Ultima*—Rudolfo Anaya
*The Color Purple*—Alice Walker
*The Red Badge of Courage*—Stephen Crane
*What Happened to Lani Garver*—Carol Plum-Ucci

**AUTHOR STUDY: TONI MORRISON**

*Beloved*
*The Bluest Eye*
*Song of Solomon*
*Sula*

**GENRE STUDY: MEMOIR**

*Colors of the Mountain*—Da Chen
*Falling Leaves: Memoir of an Unwanted Chinese Daughter*—
    Adeline Yen Mah
*The Guinness Book of Me: A Memoir of Record*—Steven Church
*I Know Why the Caged Bird Sings*—Maya Angelou
*Narrative of the Life of Frederick Douglass*—Frederick Douglass

## Twelfth Grade

**THEME: ROAD TRIPS**

*Caramelo*—Sandra Cisneros
*Caucasia*—Danzy Senna
*The Fellowship of the Ring*—J. R. R. Tolkien
*On the Road*—Jack Kerouac
*Postcards from No Man's Land*—Aidan Chambers

**THEME: KEEPING THE FAITH**

*The Chosen*—Chaim Potok
*Imani All Mine*—Connie Porter
*Life of Pi*—Yann Martel
*The Poisonwood Bible*—Barbara Kingsolver
*Siddhartha*—Herman Hesse

**GENRE STUDY: UTOPIAS/DYSTOPIAS**

*1984*—George Orwell
*Feed*—M. T. Anderson
*The Handmaid's Tale*—Margaret Atwood
*Herland*—Charlotte Perkins Gilman
*Jurassic Park*—Michael Crichton

**AUTHOR STUDY: VIRGINIA WOOLF**

*Moments of Being*
*Orlando*
*A Room of One's Own*
*Three Guineas*
*The Waves*

# Appendix B

*Resources for Record Keeping*

## CONTENTS

# B–1 Our Book Club Goals and Ground Rules

Book You're Reading: _____

Members of Your Group: _____

Name for Your Group (Create one! ☺) _____

Today's Discussion Leader: _____

Today's Scribe: _____

**GOALS:** Talk about what an ideal book club looks like to you, and then set some goals (probably no more than three or four) to make that happen for your group. List these goals below:

1. _____

2. _____

3. _____

4. _____

**GROUND RULES:** You'll have about half the period for your book club sessions each time. How do you want that time to go? Below, make a short list of ground rules (probably no more than four or five) describing the expectations you have for one another in terms of preparation and participation. Some questions to consider include the following:

◈ How do you expect people to prepare for book club?

◈ How do you want the discussion to go?

◈ How can you make sure people treat each other with honor and respect?

◈ What should your group do when someone isn't following these ground rules?

1. _____

2. _____

3. _____

4. _____

5. _____

**SIGNATURES:** By signing below, you indicate your willingness to abide by the above agreement.

# B–2 Book Club Discussion Record

Date: _____ Book Title: _____ Group Name: _____

Group Discussion Leader: _____ Scribe: _____
(Please choose a different person for each session.)     (Please choose a different person for each session.)

Other Group Members Present: _____

Group Members Absent: _____

**MAIN IDEAS GENERATED FROM BOOK CLUB MEMBERS:** Please write a one-sentence summary of the most significant ideas or questions contributed by each book club member. Write the group member's name beside her/his idea or question.

1. _____

2. _____

3. _____

4. _____

5. _____

6. _____

Today's Question(s):




Your Conclusions:

Date: _____

Class: _____

| Observations | Reflections |
|---|---|
| ◈ What's happening here? | ◈ What do I think about it? What questions does it raise? |

### To Think About

What are my overall impressions of today's book club session? What do I need to think about further? Are any needs, patterns, or questions consistently emerging? Do I need to take any specific action before the next book club session?

# Appendix C

*Top Ten Response Tools*

## CONTENTS

# C–1 ,/?/! (The Punctuation Prompt)

This response tool uses common punctuation marks to prompt your reactions to three important passages or ideas you choose in the text. You'll use your response to fuel your book club discussion. Here's how to pull it off:

1. *While you're reading*, look for **three** passages or central ideas that make you do the following:

   ◈ Give you pause or make you stop and think. Use a *comma* ( , ) to mark this passage with a sticky note.

   ◈ Cause you to wonder or ask a question. Use a *question mark* ( ? ) to mark this passage with a sticky note.

   ◈ Provoke a strong reaction of some kind. Use an *exclamation point* ( ! ) to mark this passage with a sticky note.

2. *After you've finished reading*, go back to these passages and write about why they affected you in these ways. Use the following format to record your reactions:

   ◈ Use the punctuation mark as your heading.

   ◈ Record the chapter number, page numbers, and a brief excerpt from the passage *or* briefly record the central idea you want to discuss.

   ◈ Write your response below. You may want to use these sentence stems to get you started.

   ,—This passage made me stop and think because . . .

   ?—When I read this passage, I wondered . . .

   !—I reacted strongly to this part of the text because . . .

## Sample Response to Pride and Prejudice, *by Jane Austen*

**,**

Ch. 1—*It is a truth universally known . . . in want of a wife.*—p. 11

I know this is the very first sentence of a book, but it made me stop and think about how different this time period is from today. Back then, if a man had a lot of money, he was assumed to be looking for a wife, but these days, that isn't always how it is. This sentence also makes me think the book is going to focus on marriage and money.

**?**

Why is Mrs. Bennet so obsessed with getting her daughters married? She seems to care about this more than she cares about their happiness. Are they really poor and she would get some of the money or something? Is Mr. Bennet unable to work for a living?

**!**

Ch. 5—*"I would not dance with him if I were you."*—p. 31

Thank goodness! Mrs. Bennet says this to Lizzy after Mr. Darcy insulted her at the ball. He is such a jerk! But he's also very rich, so this comment makes me think that Mrs. B. does actually care about Lizzy's happiness.

# C–2 1-2-3-Predict

Name _____ Book Title and Page Numbers _____

| | |
|:--|:--|
| **1** | **2** |

This event was important because …

_____

_____

_____

This event was important because …

_____

_____

_____

| | |
|:--|:--|
| **3** | **PREDICT** |

This event was important because …

_____

_____

_____

_____

I predict this will happen next because …

_____

_____

_____

_____

## C–3 Dailies

**Dailies** are four-column journal entries, two of which you keep *while reading*, one that you keep *during book club discussion*, and one that you complete *after book club discussion*. Dailies are your ticket into class on book club days because they will provide the starting point for your discussions. Because Dailies help you keep track of your evolving interpretations and book club discussions, I think you will find them to be extremely helpful for your final project. As usual, I'll be evaluating your Dailies for thoughtfulness, thoroughness, and completion. The format for Dailies is as follows:

1. *Heading*: Write your name and the date.

2. *Columns 1 and 2*: **Before class,** this is where you record your responses to the assigned reading. As you read, note page numbers and/or specific phrases of passages that strike you as important. Then simply respond to those passages in everyday language. Remember that you are *writing to learn* and your primary audience is yourself; but your fellow book club members and I will be "eavesdropping," so your responses will need to be complete enough that we can follow what you're saying. To get full credit for your Dailies, *you must at least fill Column 1 completely*. See the suggestions below if you need some help figuring out what to write.

3. *Column 3*: **During class,** use this column to record the highlights of that day's book club discusssion.

4. *Column 4*: **After class,** use this column to reflect on what has/hasn't changed in your thinking about this text as a result of your book club discussion. Also record any key items that might prepare you for the final project.

### Suggestions for the First Two Columns of Dailies

If you've chosen a passage that you know is important but you're having difficulty getting your response started, the following prompts can help:

⊛ My first reactions to this part of the reading are . . .

⊛ I wonder what this means. . . . It might be that . . .

- This part is confusing because . . .

- This makes me think that . . . will happen later because . . .

- The most important event/word/phrase/image/idea in this part is . . . because . . .

- This character/event/idea reminds me of . . .

- I didn't expect the character to act/react this way because . . .

- Sometimes I feel just like this character when . . .

- The characters seem to feel . . . about . . .

- This description makes me feel . . .

- The setting gives the effect of . . .

- This detail seems important/effective/out of place because . . .

- This passage is particularly effective/depressing/surprising because . . .

- This passage seems to be a pivot point because . . .

- I saw this pattern in this part of the reading . . .

- This section reminds me of the unit theme because . . .

- I imagine this character to be the sort of person who . . .

- I imagine this narrator to be the sort of person who . . .

- I imagine the author to be the sort of person who . . .

- I need to find out more about . . .

- I thought I understood . . . , but now I know . . . (Note: This prompt would also work well in Column 4!)

Another option is to ask a *real question*, that is, one you don't actually know the answer to. If you choose this option, also begin thinking on paper in response to your own question (in other words, don't just list the question and move on to the next topic). If it is indeed a real question, you probably won't come to any firm conclusions, but your thoughts will serve as a starting point so that your book club can consider possible answers together.

*Dailies*

Name: _____   Date: _____

| What I Think | What I Think (continued) | What My Book Club Thinks | What I Think Now |
|---|---|---|---|
| | | | |

# C–4 Mind Map Reading Log

Name: _____

Section of the Book (page numbers): _____

Character: _____

If you could climb inside this character's head, what do you think you'd find?

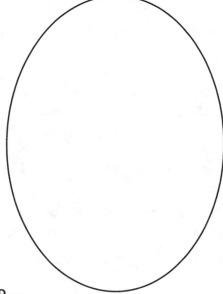

**INSIDE THE HEAD . . .**

❧ Draw three symbols or images.

❧ Record the three most important words in the story.


**ON THE BACK OF THIS PAGE . . .**

❧ Make a legend for your map, briefly explaining what each of the three symbols represents and why you chose those three words.


**IN THE SPACE BELOW . . .**

❧ Write three real questions you still have about this part of the book.

1. _____

2. _____

3. _____

## C–5 Picture This Instructions

If you made your book into a movie, what images would show up on the screen? Picture This is designed to help you visualize and reflect on what you're reading and then to promote discussion based on the images your book club members record.

### Instructions

1. *While you're reading*, mark passages that strike you as good material for your sketch.

2. *After you've read*, sketch a significant scene or image from the text in the box on the back of this page. The sketch can represent a literal event in the reading, or it can be more symbolic in nature, but it should be something you want to write about and talk about more in book club. Don't worry; the quality of the artwork isn't the point here. What matters is what you have to write and say about it. In fact, stick figures are fine.

3. *After you're finished drawing*, explain how this image is significant in the space below your sketch. Consider questions like the following:

   ◈ How did you decide what to sketch?

   ◈ Is it something that actually happened in the reading? If so, why was it so important?

   ◈ If your sketch is symbolic, what does it represent?

   ◈ What did your sketch help you understand about the reading, or what questions did it raise?

   ◈ What else do you want to say?

# Picture This

Your Sketch

Your Reflection on Your Sketch

## C–6 Q & R *(Quotation and Response)*

Sometimes you know you really like part of a book, and sometimes you know you really don't. Sometimes what you read really made you think, but you may not be sure exactly why. Q & Rs are meant to help you explore the big ideas raised by your book club book and your reactions to them. You'll use your Q & R entries to guide your book club discussion.

### Instructions

1. *While you're reading*, mark passages that strike you as important.

2. Draw a line down the center of your page. Label the left-hand column "Q" and the right-hand column "R."

3. Choose three to four of the most striking quotations you've marked and then record and respond to these quotations in the format of a double-entry journal, as described below:

**LEFT COLUMN: COMPELLING QUOTATION—**Your goal on this side of the page is to record quotations from the reading that you have found to be particularly thought provoking, baffling, or insightful. There's no need to copy the entire quotation. Excerpts are fine as long as they capture a sense of the passage. *Be sure to record the page numbers* so you can refer back to the passages during book club discussion.

**RIGHT COLUMN: RESPONSE TO THE QUOTATION—**On this side of the page, respond to each quotation in any fashion that helps you make better sense of it. Your goal is to succintly explore your reactions to this quotation, using one of the following options:

    a. *Question*—Write a real question *designed to extend the thinking of the rest of your book club* in response to this quotation in particular or to a related concept in the reading selection as a whole. Try to begin working out an answer on paper.

    b. *Accept*—Specifically explain why you agree with this quotation and how you find the ideas expressed there to be compelling.

    c. *Resist*—Problematize the quotation by describing which parts of it are appealing and challenging those that seem unlikely to you.

    d. *Ignore*—If this quotation goes against every fiber of your being, tell yourself why.

Regardless of your choice among these four options, be sure to use everyday language since you are *writing to learn*. As long as your responses are honest, they cannot be wrong.

| Q | R |
|---|---|
|   |   |

# C–7 Reading Logs

In an effort to do some educated reading, you will keep a Reading Log on notebook paper as you read your book club book. The Reading Log will help you do the following:

- think *while* you are reading
- determine the course of your book club discussions
- prepare you for your final project on your book club book

The Reading Logs will be graded *for completion only*. To get full credit, however, your log must meet these requirements:

- You must indicate the page number for each quotation you have chosen.
- Your choice of quotations and your reactions to them *must be original*. In other words, no borrowing from your neighbor.
- You must complete *at least a one-page log for each reading assignment*.

## INSTRUCTIONS

For each segment of your book club book, divide one piece of notebook paper into two columns by folding your paper in half vertically, opening it back up, and then drawing a line down the center of the page. *On the left side of the page, write down quotations that caught your attention while you were reading*—lines or passages that appealed to you, confused you, made you react strongly, or really made you think. Don't feel as if you have to copy down the entire passage if it's a long one. Instead, list the first few lines, write an ellipsis (. . .), and list the last few lines that conclude the passage. Just be sure to list enough to give a sense of the passage as I demonstrated in class.

*For each quotation you list on the left, write your comments and/or questions about the quotation on the right side of the page*. Perhaps you will draw a conclusion *or* make a connection between this passage and something else. If you have trouble getting started, the following prompts can help:

- My first reactions to this text are . . .
- I wonder what this means . . . It might be that . . .

- This character/passage/text reminds me of . . .
- This part is confusing because . . .
- This passage made me feel . . . I reacted this way because . . .
- The most important word/phrase/event/image/idea in this text is . . . because . . .
- The most difficult word/image/concept in this text is . . . because . . .
- The title of this text or chapter seems (in)significant because . . .
- I didn't expect the character to do this/react in this way because . . .
- I agree/disagree with the ideas in this section of the text because . . .
- The language in this section seems important because . . .
- I imagine this character/narrator/author to be the sort of person who . . .
- I need to know/hear/find out more about . . .
- Sometimes I feel just like this character when . . .
- This makes me think that . . . will happen later because . . .
- I thought I understood . . . , but now I understand . . .

*Questions are also fine*, but if you ask one, I'd like for you to try to begin working out some hunches on paper. If it's a real question, you probably won't be able to answer it fully. That's OK because when you bring the question to class, the rest of us will take a look at your hunches so far and go from there.

Think and write *as you read* rather than waiting till the end of your reading assignment, when you might forget what it was you wanted to say. If you find that this disrupts the flow of your reading too much, you may simply want to note the pages with interesting passages and go back and write about them when you're finished reading. Concentrate on getting your ideas down on paper rather than being too concerned about whether or not the writing is perfect. Phrases are fine because you'll be using them to prompt your conversation in class. The only way to mess up on this assignment is to simply summarize the passage on the right side of the page. Instead, I want to see your *reactions* to what you've read. Listen for your own voice, trust what it's telling you, and you'll be fine. Find out what you have to say about what you have read.

©2006 by Cindy O'Donnell-Allen from *The Book Club Companion*. Portsmouth, NH: Heinemann.

# C–8 Real Books Letters

## Questions and Answers

Dear Wonderful English Students (yes, this does mean you):

This is my promised attempt to explain to you just what a Real Books (RB) Letter is. You will write one RB Letter for each part of the book as designated below and will address your letters to your book club.

Each letter must be a **minimum of two pages long** (i.e., I want to see *letters*, not *postcards*) and should consist of your personal, thoughtful response to the reading. I want you to write/think on paper in **your voice**, primarily for **your own benefit** in discovering what **you** know about this book. Just think of your book club members and me as friendly eavesdroppers on your thoughts, and dazzle us with your brilliance. An easy task, right?

The only way to mess up this assignment is to simply summarize your book club book's events. I know you can understand what you read. I want to see what you thought about it. Oh, and be sure to include ideas from several places in the assigned reading. So just what do you write in your letters? Here are a few helpful hints to ensure your success on this assignment. In each of your letters, you must include the following *required* items:

1. A *discussion of the single most significant* **event** *or* **line** *for this section of your reading*—How is this event or line important to the book as a whole? Why do you think the author included it? What does it add to the book?

2. A *discussion of the book's relationship to the* **unit theme**—How do the characters relate to the theme for this unit? Why would you describe the character or characters in this way?

3. A *reflection on your* **reading processes**—What do you do as you're reading? What did you think about and what did you see as you read this section of the book? What strategies help you understand this section of the book? What, if anything, do you find to be fascinating or difficult about the overall process of reading? In this section, provide information that will acquaint the rest of your group with your habits, strategies, and processes.

4. *PS—After* you've completed your two pages, record **five interesting words** from this section of your book as a postscript (PS), and tell us why you chose them. If these words are unfamiliar, provide a

definition. If they aren't unfamiliar, simply tell us why you chose them anyway. For instance, you might like the way the author used the word in an unusual way, or you might appreciate the strong image the word creates. This practice might not only spill over into your own writing but could also help you win friends and influence people with your reputation as a *logophile* (speaking of new words . . .). Gee, aren't you glad you took this class?

## So What Do I Say for the Rest of My Letter?

As mentioned above, each letter must be a **minimum of two pages long**. If you have not reached this minimum after responding to requirements 1–3, you may write about anything but just the plot alone. Your book club will use your letters to fuel your discussion over the book and to help with final projects later on. So include pressing questions, comments, and concerns that represent your best thinking about the book. **Always** come to book club with something to say. Here are a few suggestions:

◈ Write personal responses to the work. Discuss your thoughts, feelings, reactions, and so on. Tell what you like and/or dislike, and be sure to explain why. What is confusing or unusual? Which character fascinates you? What do you think will happen next? Well, you get the idea.

◈ Occasionally relate situations, characters, ideas, setting, and so on to personal experience or to someone you know. Or relate them to other texts (books, plays, TV, movies, songs, etc.).

◈ Ask questions, questions, questions, and try to puzzle the answers out on paper.

◈ Discuss the author's style of writing. We don't want all those discussions of literary techniques to go to waste now, do we? How does the author use language to achieve the effects of the passages that move you?

After you get the hang of writing them, I think you'll really enjoy RB Letters because they will allow you to *write to learn* what you think about the novel, rather than start from someone else's agenda. As long as your letter is thoughtfully written and represents your personal response to the book, you will get full credit. So relax, get conversational, and enjoy this assignment. I'm looking forward to reading the results!

## How to Make Your Sticky Notes Bookmark

1. Use your scissors to cut along the outer edges of your bookmark.

2. Fold the whole bookmark in half *vertically* so that the printed part is on the *inside*. In other words, the open edges will be on the *right*, and you won't be able to see the print. When you open your bookmark back up, it will now have an "invisible" fold line down the middle.

3. Once you've opened your bookmark back up, the next step is to make folds on the *printed* vertical lines that form the columns. But this time, fold the printed parts to the *outside* so that one column is overlapping the other. At this point, your bookmark should be the shape of a candy bar.

4. Now open the bookmark back up, and fold it down the middle "invisible" vertical line again. But this time, fold it the opposite way that you did before so that the printed part is on the *outside*. In other words, the open edges will be on the left, and you can still see all the print.

5. Tape the outer open edges together only on the left side. *Do not tape the top and bottom edges!* These will remain open for a reason.

6. Now press the inside printed folds of the bookmark back into the middle so that it looks sort of like a hot dog bun.

7. You're finished! On one side of the "bun," you should be able to see "Your Official Sticky Notes Bookmark" and your reading schedule. On the other side of the bun, you can see your "Sticky Notes Reminders." But if you open up the bookmark to look inside the bun, you can still read the "What's Up with the Sticky Notes?" part in the middle where the hot dog would be.

| Your Official **Sticky Notes** Bookmark | What's Up with the Sticky Notes? | Sticky Notes Reminders |
|---|---|---|
| **READING SCHEDULE**<br><br>By _____,<br><br>read to p. _____.<br><br><br>By _____,<br><br>read to p. _____.<br><br><br>By _____,<br><br>read to p. _____.<br><br><br>By _____,<br><br>read to p. _____. | Since you chose this book, the hard part probably won't be reading it. The hard part will be stopping! But . . .<br><br>You've agreed to talk about it! So you need to stop every so often and think about the parts that will help you remember what you think is important. And . . .<br><br>That's where the sticky notes come in. They'll remind you to mark the parts you'd like to talk about in book club without slowing down your reading too much.<br><br>So here's how to use them:<br><br>1. When you come to a part that you'd like to talk more about in book club, peel off a sticky note to mark the page.<br><br>2. Use the reminders in the next column ➤ to help you decide why you chose this part in the first place.<br><br>3. Then, write down a short reminder for yourself directly on the sticky note.<br><br>When you get back to book club, you'll use your sticky notes to help you decide what to talk about. That's all there is to it! | *Did you see that?*<br>   We should talk about this part because . . .<br><br>*This part reminds me...*<br>   I can relate to this part because . . .<br><br>*I just don't get it...*<br>   I had a question about this part because . . .<br><br>*Thinking Cap Required*<br>   This part really made me think because . . .<br><br>*Crystal Ball Required*<br>   I bet this will happen next . . .<br><br>*WWYD?*<br>   What would you do in the same situation?<br><br>*If I were the author . . .*<br>   I would've written this instead . . .<br><br>*Say anything.*<br>   Respond however you'd like.<br><br>*Ask anything.*<br>   Ask whatever you want.<br><br>*Create your own prompt.*<br><br>   1. _____<br><br>   2. _____<br><br>   3. _____ |

| Your Official *Textual Approach* Bookmark | What's Up with the Sticky Notes? | Sticky Notes Prompts |
|---|---|---|
| **The Textual Perspective Defined**<br><br>The reader examines patterns among the structural elements of a text in order to construct meaning.<br><br>## READING SCHEDULE<br><br>By _____,<br><br>read to p. _____.<br><br><br>By _____,<br><br>read to p. _____.<br><br><br>By _____,<br><br>read to p. _____.<br><br><br>By _____,<br><br>read to p. _____. | In the next column, you'll see a list of questions typical of the textual approach. Because this approach focuses on the same kind of close reading you've most likely done in prior English classes, applying it will probably feel pretty familiar to you.<br><br>So as you're reading and reviewing your book club book, a good way to use your sticky notes is to mark passages where you find yourself attending to such textual elements as *character, plot, setting, theme, point of view, style, tone,* and *symbols.* Be sure to jot down a "note to self" on the sticky note so you'll remember the question/comment/concern that prompted you to mark the passage in the first place.<br><br>On book club days, you'll use these sticky notes to focus your discussion and to reflect on the processes involved in applying a textual perspective in your reading. | *Character:* What do the characters do, say, think, feel, especially in regard to the emerging conflict? What clues do these actions/words/thoughts/feelings give you about each character's personality, motives, and expectations? Is the character *round/dynamic* or *flat/static*? What were each character's defining moments? What did you or the characters expect? What did you get?<br><br>*Plot:* Does the story follow a traditional pattern (i.e., beginning, middle, end)? *If so,* where does the story *really* begin? What events lead to and mark particular pivot points? How are conflicts resolved? *If not,* what patterns of narration does the author employ (e.g., flashbacks, foreshadowing, suspense building, etc.)? What traditional elements of narration are changed? How do these changes affect the story's meaning?<br><br>*Setting:* How does the setting affect the characters? The story's/narrator's credibility?<br><br>*Theme:* What's the story's universal subject? What does the author have to say about that subject?<br><br>*Point of View:* Who tells the story? How does this perspective influence the telling?<br><br>*Style/tone/symbols:* How does the writer express her/himself? What words does he/she choose? To what effect? Are there any words or objects that have meaning beyond themselves? |

# C–12 Sticky Notes Bookmark—Social

| Your Official *Social Approach* Bookmark | What's Up with the Sticky Notes? | Sticky Notes Prompts |
|---|---|---|
| **The Social Perspective Defined**<br><br>Readers define their social relationship with the text by evaluating (1) the writer's motives for telling the story, (2) the sources of characters' behaviors and relationships, and (3) the sources of readers' own responses.<br><br><br>## READING SCHEDULE<br><br><br>By _____,<br><br>read to p. _____.<br><br><br><br>By _____,<br><br>read to p. _____.<br><br><br><br>By _____,<br><br>read to p. _____.<br><br><br><br>By _____,<br><br>read to p. _____. | In the next column, you'll see a list of questions typical of the social approach. These are written in academic language, but the heart of the social approach is *relationships*— between you and the characters, the characters and one another, and the author and her/his implied audience.<br><br>So as you review your book club text, a good way to use your sticky notes is to mark passages where<br><br>• you find yourself relating in some way, be it positive or negative, to<br><br>  – a particular character<br><br>  – particular relationships (e.g., friendships, families, couples, etc.)<br><br>  – a particular social situation<br><br>*or*<br><br>• you see the characters relating to one another in a significant, surprising, or predictable way<br><br>*or*<br><br>• you find yourself relating in some way, be it positive or negative, to the author's perspective or possible motives for telling this story | • Do I identify with the author's implied audience or not (e.g., Would I be a likely friend for this author or the book's characters? Why or why not?)?<br>• What are the author's possible social motives for telling this story? To illustrate a point? Dramatize a problem? Impress an audience? Something else? How are these motives illustrated through characters' thoughts, conversations, and other behaviors?<br>• How do I feel about these characters? Close or distant? How do they feel about each other and about themselves? Did my relationships with certain characters change in the course of the story? Why?<br>• What role does language play in defining and creating the social relationships in this story? Is a speaker's or character's language formal, informal, academic, or colloquial? How do these differences in language convey social roles or imply social relationships within the text? How do they affect my relationship with the author and the characters?<br>• What social conventions are conveyed through the setting(s) of the story? How do these conventions shape and reveal characters' attitudes and behaviors?<br>• Do I find the story's resolution to be just or not? How has my opinion been affected by my judgments of characters?<br>• What is my overall reaction to this text as I read? Do I feel detached? Spellbound? Skeptical? Trusting? Fulfilled? What are the sources of this reaction?<br>• How is my understanding of this text shaped by my own social attitudes, values, and experiences? By others' reactions? |

| Your Official **Topical Approach** Bookmark | What's Up with the Sticky Notes? | Sticky Notes Prompts |
|---|---|---|
| **The Topical Perspective Defined**<br><br>Readers apply their background knowledge of different fields or topics to their understanding of a text. This approach encourages an intertextual perspective.<br><br>### READING SCHEDULE<br><br>By _____,<br><br>read to p. _____.<br><br><br>By _____,<br><br>read to p. _____.<br><br><br>By _____,<br><br>read to p. _____.<br><br><br>By _____,<br><br>read to p. _____. | In the next column, you'll see a list of questions typical of the topical approach. All of the books we are reading for this book club are focused on the topic of _____.<br><br>So **before** you read your book club book, you'll need to broaden your knowledge of<br><br>_____<br><br>in general since that's the topic you'll be examining in conjunction with your book club book. To do so, I'm asking you to surf **one** of the following websites and take notes on **or** print out interesting material you find there so that you can share your findings with your book club.<br><br>Website Addresses:<br><br><br><br>Once you've done your Internet research, use your sticky notes to mark passages as suggested by the prompts in the next column. | • What *fields* (e.g., history, science, art, music, ethics, etc.) or *topics* (e.g., censorship, the West, war, race relations, small-town life, religious backgrounds, rites of passage, background of the author, etc.) are relevant to understanding this text?<br>• What do I already know in regard to these fields or topics that helps me understand this text? Based on these facts, what generalizations can I make? How do these generalizations apply to this text?<br>• How does this text confirm or contradict what I know or believe about these fields or topics?<br>• What are the relationships among these fields and topics? How do other texts portray the same topic or field differently?<br>• What *more* do I need to know about these fields or topics to better understand this text? How can I find out (e.g., research, interviewing experts in the field, etc.)? How has my understanding of the text changed as a result of acquiring this knowledge?<br>• How might assuming a particular perspective affect my perceptions of this text? (I.e., if I were to read this text as a _____ [historian, scientist, lawyer, journalist, publisher, teacher, etc.], what conclusions would I draw?) How has my understanding of the text changed as a result of adopting this perspective? |

## C–14 Sticky Notes Bookmark—Cultural

| Your Official **Cultural Approach** Bookmark | What's Up with the Sticky Notes? | Sticky Notes Prompts |
|---|---|---|
| **The Cultural Perspective Defined** Readers examine how the expectations, values, and conventions of different institutional or cultural forces shape the text itself as well as readers' responses to and understanding of that text. **READING SCHEDULE** By _____, read to p. _____. By _____, read to p. _____. By _____, read to p. _____. By _____, read to p. _____. | This time, you'll actually *wait* to use your sticky notes until your book club has selected a specific subject from one of the categories below that you wish to examine in the book. Once you've decided on a subject, you'll use your sticky notes as you review your book club book to simply mark places in the book where that subject appears. You'll then use these references as evidence for your cultural studies presentation. The categories below refer to different institutional or cultural forces, while the items in parentheses are subjects you might consider: <br>• **traditional and nontraditional texts** (such as film, TV, ads, oral histories, magazines, newspapers, lyrics, and music videos) <br>• **social institutions** (such as family, school, workplace, peer group, the arts) <br>• **social distinctions** (such as gender, race, religion, education, ethnicity, class) <br>So what can you do in the meantime? Think about the categories above and begin making a list of interesting subjects that appear in your book club book so that your book club will have several subjects from which to choose. | • What social and cultural forces (e.g., peer groups, mass media, family, school, region, historical period, language; religious, social, or political communities; class, race, ethnicity, gender) appear to have shaped the author's rendering of this text? What social, economic, and political interests does the text serve? <br>• How are the characters shaped by these social and cultural forces? Are they positive forces that encourage growth, negative forces that discourage it, or somewhere in between? How do characters accept/reject/subvert/transcend the values imposed by these cultural forces? What values (for the character *and* in the text) emerge as a result? <br>• How do these social and cultural forces overlap, and how are they in conflict with one another? What central oppositions exist? How do these overlaps/oppositions illuminate the culture constructed by the text? <br>• How might your overall reactions to this text have been influenced by your class, gender, ethnicity, particular background? <br>• How are the characters in this novel portrayed? What roles are characters free to assume or prevented from assuming? What value assumptions appear to shape these portrayals (e.g., women in Shakespeare versus women in Chopin)? <br>• How is your response affected when you "read through" the text as opposed to when you "read against" it? <br>• How are the social and cultural forces of your book club book portrayed in other cultural texts? |

The main audience for the exploratory writing you'll be completing for book clubs is you, yourself. Because these entries are exploratory in nature, you are writing to discover what you think. Or as E. M. Forster once put it: "How do I know what I think until I see what I say?" Your other audiences consist of friendly eavesdroppers—the other members of your book club and me.

I use a checkpoint system to evaluate your responses so that I can return them to you quickly and so that you'll know how you're doing along the way. Occasionally, I'll just give you credit (a check) for completion, but usually you'll find one of the following symbols at the top of the page. Here's what they mean:

✓ : You earn a check when you complete the minimum requirements listed on the assignment sheet in a *thoughtful and thorough* manner. Even though the piece is exploratory, your writing is clear enough that I can easily understand your ideas.

✓+ : You earn a check-plus when you go above and beyond the minimum requirements in some way. Perhaps you've arrived at some especially insightful conclusion, raised a compelling question, or have stated your claims in particularly well-fashioned terms. In other words, you've taken great care in what you've said and how you've said it, and it shows.

✓– : You earn a check-minus when one or more of the following problems exists: You haven't met the minimum requirements of the assignment. Your response feels neither *thoughtful nor thorough*. Instead, it feels like you're simply going through the motions. Your writing is so unclear that I can't understand the gist of what you're saying.

My written comments, when I make them (and I won't always, though I *will* always read what you've written), will usually be more "readerly" than "graderly." In other words, I'll try to respond to what you've said by telling you when and how you've made me think or by pushing you to keep thinking, usually by raising questions you might not have considered. Probably the only time I'll fall into a graderly mode is when you've earned a check-minus so that you'll know how to avoid similar problems in future entries.

# Appendix D

*Final Four Assessment Tools and Scoring Guides*

## CONTENTS

# D–1 Life Map Presentation

For this project, your group will create a Life Map, capturing the most significant features in the life of your book club book. Your Life Map must include

◈ eight to ten visual images, symbolizing the prominent features of your book (ex.: important events, characters, symbols, themes)

◈ the three most important lines from your book

◈ any additional elements you deem appropriate

You will have some workshop time to prepare in class, but to make good use of it, you will need to come with a plan, which is where your last book club discussion comes in. During this discussion, you'll need to make a list of potential Life Map elements in each of the required categories for the purposes of guiding your group's work on the Life Map. You'll undoubtedly come up with more ideas during workshop time, but keep in mind that the more you decide on during your last book club discussion, the more you'll be able to accomplish in class.

Your Life Map presentations should be no more than ten minutes in length and should inspire an additional five minutes of question-and-answer discussion about your book. As usual, I will expect *all* group members to contribute equally in all phases of the project—thinking, planning, discussing, constructing, and presenting. On the day of your presentation, you should give me a job list with each group member's name and the tasks he or she was responsible for.

Your goals are to

◈ provide an engaging, thought-provoking overview of the life of your book by introducing us to its prominent features

◈ carefully defend the significance of the three most important lines you selected

◈ answer questions that the class has about your book

## Some Ideas to Consider as You Plan Your Life Map

1. Considering the fact that the narrator does not document every day in the life of your book's characters, take a look at what he or she *has* chosen to recount. In terms of both plot and character, what are the *most important events*, and how are they significant to the book's development as a whole?

2. What role does the *setting* play in the book? How does it contribute to the larger purposes/big ideas of the book?

3. What do the *central characters* learn? How do they change? What are their defining moments, and what do they realize from them? Who are they, really? What do they want from life? From every day? Do they deserve what they get?

4. What are the *main conflicts* in the book? What causes them? How are they resolved? How do they develop the book's *theme(s)*?

5. What influence does the narrator's *point of view* have on the book? Toward which characters are you sympathetic? Which characters do you dislike? Do you consider the narrator's version of the story to be reliable? How might the story change if it were told from another point of view?

6. What do you consider to be the *three most important lines* in the book? Record these somewhere on your Life Map and analyze them in your presentation. How and why do these lines affect you as readers?

7. Are there important *images or symbols* in your book? If so, what purposes do they serve, and how might you represent them on your Life Map?

8. Aside from these questions, what *other elements* feature significantly in your book? How can you include them?

**DON'T FORGET TO CONSIDER** . . . the importance of color and placement as symbolic features when you determine where to position things on your Life Map.

# Life Map Presentation Scoring Guide

Group Members: _____

Book Title: _____

## Presentation includes these required elements:

- eight to ten visual images, symbolizing the prominent features of the book (ex.: important events, characters, symbols, themes)
- the three most important lines from the book
- any additional elements _____

## Presentation meets these goals:

- provides an engaging, thought-provoking overview of the life of the book by introducing us to its prominent features
- carefully defends the significance of the three most important lines of the book
- answers questions that the class has about the book

## Group demonstrates these effective preparation and presentation skills:

- makes good use of workshop time
- speaks clearly at an appropriate pace and volume
- uses an appropriate and engaging format
- appears comfortable with presentation content

## Group has invested time and care in the preparation of the presentation so that the group:

- seems polished
- uses time efficiently (plans wisely for ten-minute time limit)
- provides required materials (Life Map, participation statement listing each member's role and signed by all members)

## Comments:

Life Map Grade: _____

# D–2 The Body Biography Presentation

For the protagonist of your book club book, your group will be creating a Body Biography—a visual and written portrait illustrating several aspects of the character's life.

The first step is to decide which of you is willing to lie down on your giant sheet of butcher paper so that the others can trace the outline of your body. Then you have many possibilities for filling up this outline. I have listed several, but please feel free to come up with your own creations. The choices you make should be based on the text, for you will be verbally explaining (and thus, in a sense, defending) them at a showing of your work. Above all, your choices should be creative, thought provoking, and analytical.

You will have some workshop time in class to prepare your Body Biography. After completing it, you will participate in a showing in which you will present your masterpiece to the class. This showing should accomplish several objectives. It should

- communicate to us the full essence of the protagonist by emphasizing the traits that make her or him who she or he is

- review your protagonist's guiding motives for the significant choices he or she makes and the changes he or she undergoes in the book

- introduce us to the central relationships, social issues, and ethical questions raised in your book club book

- describe your group's overall reaction to the book, including your thoughts on how your attitudes, values, and experiences might have shaped that reaction

## Body Biography Requirements

Although I expect that your Body Biography will contain additional elements, you are *required* to include the following:

- a review of significant choices, changes, and relationships in the book

- visual symbols

- the three most important lines uttered by or about your protagonist

- an original text (ex.: free-verse poem, diary entry, news article, letter, etc.)

## Body Biography Suggestions

1. *Placement*—Carefully choose the placement of your text and artwork. For example, the area where your protagonist's heart would be might be appropriate for illustrating the important relationships within his or her life.

2. *Spine*—Actors often discuss a character's spine. This is her or his main objective within the play. What is the most important goal for your protagonist? What drives her or his thoughts and actions? This is her or his spine. How can you illustrate it?

3. *Virtues and Vices*—What are your protagonist's most admirable qualities? Her or his worst? How can you make us visualize them? What social issues and ethical questions do these virtues and vices raise?

4. *Color*—Colors are often symbolic. What color(s) do you most associate with your protagonist? Why? How can you effectively work these colors into your presentation?

5. *Symbols*—How might you represent your protagonist's essential self in purely visual terms? Are there objects mentioned within the novel itself that you could use? If not, choose objects that especially seem to correspond with the protagonist.

6. *Perspective*—What influence does the narrator's point of view have on the book? Toward which characters are you sympathetic? Which characters do you dislike? Do you find the narrator's version of the truth to be believable? It might be useful for you to consider how the story would change if it were told from another narrator's point of view.

7. *Mirror, Mirror*—Consider both how your protagonist appears to others on the surface and what you know about her or his inner self. Do these images clash or correspond? What does this tell you about the character?

8. *Changes*—How has your protagonist changed in the course of the book? Trace these changes within your original text and/or artwork.

# Body Biography Presentation Scoring Guide

Group Members: _____

Book Title: _____

## Presentation includes these required elements:

◈ a review of significant choices, changes, and relationships in the book

◈ visual symbols

◈ the three most important lines uttered by or about your protagonist

◈ an original text (ex.: free-verse poem, diary entry, news article, letter, etc.)

◈ any additional elements _____

## Presentation meets these goals:

◈ communicates the full essence of the protagonist by emphasizing the traits that make her or him who she or he is

◈ reviews the protagonist's guiding motives for the significant choices he or she makes and the changes he or she undergoes

◈ introduces the central relationships, social issues, and ethical questions raised in the book

◈ describes the group's overall reaction to the book, including thoughts on how group members' attitudes, values, and experiences might have shaped that reaction

## Group demonstrates these effective presentation skills:

◈ speaks clearly at an appropriate pace and volume

◈ uses an appropriate and engaging format

◈ appears comfortable with presentation content

*Group has invested time and care in the preparation of the presentation so that the group:*

⚜ seems polished

⚜ uses workshop and presentation time efficiently (plans wisely for ten-minute time limit)

⚜ provides required materials (Body Biography, participation statement listing each member's role and signed by all members)

*Comments:*

Body Biography Grade: _____

# D–3 Censorship Scenario: Should This Book Be Saved?

Throughout this book club, we've been studying book banning and censorship. You've conducted some Internet research, used your sticky notes to mark places in your book that might be relevant to these topics, and explored your own feelings about them in book club discussions. To bring all this work together in a final project, we will imagine that the books we've been reading in book clubs have been challenged by a group of concerned community members. Before these books can be removed from the curriculum, the school board must hold a special meeting to review the community's concerns.

You will choose two members from your book club to become characters who represent opposing viewpoints on whether or not to ban your book club book. These characters will participate on a panel at the school board meeting to decide the fate of the books. Here are some roles to choose from:

- a concerned *parent* challenging the book

- the *teacher* who assigned the book

- a *school board member* who does/doesn't think censorship is a good idea

- the *author* of the book

- the school *librarian*

- the *principal*

- a *student* who does/doesn't want to read the book

- a *community member* from an (imaginary) organization called PAST (Parents Against Scandalous Texts)

On the day of the school board meeting, both of your characters will participate with panel members from other book clubs to answer the following questions:

- *Should these book club books remain in our school's curriculum?*

- *Why or why not?*

- *What are your feelings about book banning and censorship overall?*

Every character will have one minute to summarize her or his point of view before the meeting is open for discussion and questions from the audience. An orderly, respectful atmosphere will be enforced.

After the meeting, we will reflect on this experience as a class and discuss how exploring both sides of the coin has influenced your current position on censorship, banned books, and the freedom to read.

### How to Prepare

1. Review all the information on book banning and censorship that you've collected in the course of the book club and think about how each character would react to it. This includes your Internet research, your sticky notes, and your book club discussion records.

2. Make notes on the following information from each character's point of view:

   - the *pros and cons* of keeping your book club book in the school curriculum

   - *passages* from the book that support this opinion

   - this character's *recommendation* about whether or not the book should stay in the curriculum (The character may respond with a yes, no, or maybe, but he or she must justify the opinion with specific evidence and clear reasoning.)

   You will turn these notes in on the day of the school board meeting.

3. Let your book club volunteers practice discussing these notes in character as if they were at the board meeting. Provide encouragement and constructive feedback.

# Censorship Scenario Scoring Guide

Group Members: _____

Book Title: _____

## The book club has met the following goals of this project:

◈ selected two book club volunteers to become characters who represented opposing viewpoints on whether or not to ban your book
club book

◈ prepared each volunteer to answer the questions (1) Should this
book club book remain in our school's curriculum? (2) Why or
why not? (3) What are your feelings about book banning and
censorship overall?

◈ participated in a class discussion reflecting on how this project
influenced your current position on censorship, banned books,
and the freedom to read

## Book club volunteers demonstrate these effective presentation skills:

◈ speak in character at an appropriate pace and volume

◈ appear comfortable with presentation content

◈ use time efficiently to state character's viewpoint

◈ are respectful of other panel members

## Group has invested time and care in preparing for the school board meeting by:

◈ gathering material on book banning and censorship collected over
the course of the book club

◈ using workshop time efficiently

◈ generating notes for book club volunteers

◈ helping volunteers rehearse

◈ providing required materials (character notes, participation statement
listing each member's role and signed by all members)

## Comments:

Censorship Scenario Grade: _____

©2006 by Cindy O'Donnell-Allen from *The Book Club Companion*. Portsmouth, NH: Heinemann.

# D–4 Cultural Studies Project

Throughout this book club, you have examined the gender expectations and issues apparent in your book. For this project, you will prepare a fifteen-minute PowerPoint presentation analyzing how these expectations and issues are also represented in contemporary culture. Divide your presentation up into the following five-minute segments:

- *First Five Minutes:* Analyze a text of some kind that you think illustrates gender expectations and issues in contemporary society. You should identify the author and audience for this text as well as describe its intended impact.
- *Second Five Minutes:* Analyze passages from your book club that illustrate gender expectations and issues.
- *Third Five Minutes:* Describe how the outside text relates to your book club book and answer the "So what?" question. How has this project influenced your personal views on gender expectations and issues, and why?

## How to Prepare

You'll have some workshop time in class and in the computer lab to prepare for your presentation.

1. Decide on an outside text you think would be interesting to analyze. Some ideas include analyzing a teen magazine, film, TV show, piece of artwork, written text, song lyrics, or music video.
2. Refer back to your sticky notes and book club discussion records to see what you've already figured out about the gender expectations and issues in your book club book.
3. Use these questions to help you analyze both texts:
     - How does the author of this text attempt to position you as an audience member?
     - Do you find the text to be appealing and/or persuasive? Why or why not?
     - Who would be able to read this text unproblematically?
     - Whose interests does the text serve?
4. On the day of your presentation, I'll ask you to turn in an informal presentation **outline**, a **disk copy** of your PowerPoint presentation, and a **participation statement** signed by all book club members that describes how each of you helped with the presentation.

# Cultural Studies Project Scoring Guide

Group Members: _____

Book Title: _____

## Presentation includes these required elements:

◈ a five-minute analysis of a text that illustrates gender expectations and issues in contemporary society

◈ a five-minute analysis of passages from the book club book that illustrate gender expectations and issues

◈ a five-minute reflection on how and why the project has influenced group members' personal views on gender expectations and issues

## Presentation meets these goals:

◈ selects an appropriate outside text and book club passages that demonstrate gender expectations and issues

◈ provides an engaging and thought-provoking analysis of both texts

◈ addresses the "So what?" question with insight

## Group demonstrates these effective preparation and presentation skills:

◈ makes good use of workshop time

◈ speaks clearly at an appropriate pace and volume

◈ creates an engaging PowerPoint presentation

◈ appears comfortable with presentation content

## Group has invested time and care in the preparation of the presentation so that the group:

◈ seems polished

◈ uses time efficiently (plans wisely for fifteen-minute time limit)

◈ provides required materials (outline, a disk copy, and signed participation statement)

## Comments:

Cultural Studies Project Grade: _____

# References

Alvermann, D., J. Young, D. Weaver, K. Hinchman, D. Moore, S. Phelps, E. Thrash, and P. Zalewski. 1996. "Middle- and High-School Students' Perceptions of How They Experience Text-Based Discussions: A Multicase Study." *Reading Research Quarterly* 19: 244–67.

Applebee, A. N., J. A. Langer, M. Nystrand, and A. Gamoran. 2003. "Discussion-Based Approaches to Developing Understanding: Classroom Instruction and Student Performance in Middle and High School English." *American Educational Research Journal* 40: 685–730.

Appleman, D. 2000. *Critical Encounters in High School English: Teaching Literary Theory to Adolescents.* New York: Teachers College Press.

Atwell, N. 1998. *In the Middle: Reading and Writing with Adolescents.* 2d ed. Portsmouth, NH: Boynton/Cook.

Barnes, D. 1992. *From Communication to Curriculum.* 2d ed. Portsmouth, NH: Heinemann.

Barnes, D., and F. Todd. 1977. *Communication and Learning in Small Groups.* Boston: Routledge/Kegan Paul.

Beach, R., and J. Marshall. 1991. *Teaching Literature in the Secondary School.* Orlando, FL: Harcourt Brace College.

Beach, R., and J. Myers. 2001. *Inquiry-Based English Instruction: Engaging Students in Life and Literature.* New York: Teachers College Press.

Beers, K. 2003. *When Kids Can't Read, What Teachers Can Do.* Portsmouth, NH: Heinemann.

Belenky, M. F., B. M. Clinchy, N. R. Goldberger, and J. M. Tarule. 1986. *Women's Ways of Knowing: The Development of Self, Voice, and Mind.* New York: Basic.

Bigelow, T., and M. J. Vokoun. 2005. *"What Choice Do I Have?" Reading, Writing, and Speaking Activities to Empower Students.* Portsmouth, NH: Heinemann.

Cazden, C. 1988. *Classroom Discourse: The Language of Teaching and Learning.* Portsmouth, NH: Heinemann.

Christensen, L. 2000. *Reading, Writing, and Rising Up: Teaching About Social Justice and the Power of the Written Word.* Milwaukee: Rethinking Schools.

Cochran-Smith, M., and S. Lytle. 1993. *Inside/Outside: Teacher Research and Knowledge*. New York: Teachers College Press.

Colorado Department of Education. 1995. *Colorado Model Content Standards for Reading and Writing*. Retrieved May 5, 2005, from www.cde.state.co.us/index_stnd.htm.

Cullinan, B. E. 1997. Foreword. In *The Book Club Connection: Literacy, Learning, and Classroom Talk,* ed. S. McMahon and F. Raphael, ix–x. New York: Teachers College Press.

Cushman, E., E. R. Kintgen, B. M. Kroll, and M. Rose. 2001. *Literacy: A Critical Sourcebook*. New York: Bedford/St. Martin's.

Damon, W., and E. Phelps. 1989. "Critical Distinctions Among Three Approaches to Peer Education." *International Journal of Educational Review* 58 (2): 9–19.

Daniels, H. 2002. *Literature Circles: Voice and Choice in Book Clubs and Reading Groups*. 2d ed. Portland, ME: Stenhouse.

Daniels, H., and N. Steineke. 2005. *Mini-Lessons for Literature Circles*. Portsmouth, NH: Heinemann.

Edelsky, C. 1992. "A Talk with Carole Edelsky About Politics and Literacy." *Language Arts* 69 (5): 324–29.

———. 1994. "Education for Democracy." *Language Arts* 71 (4): 252–57.

Faust, M. 2005. "Half-Cultivated Fields: Teachers as Readers in University Sponsored Book Clubs." In *Student Book Clubs: Improving Literature Instruction in Middle and High School*, ed. M. Faust, J. Cockrill, C. Hancock, and H. Isserstedt, 30–71. Norwood, MA: Christopher-Gordon.

Faust, M., J. Cockrill, C. Hancock, and H. Isserstedt. 2005. Introduction. In *Student Book Clubs: Improving Literature Instruction in Middle and High School*, vii–xvii. Norwood, MA: Christopher-Gordon.

Fecho, B. 2004. *"Is This English?" Race, Language, and Culture in the Classroom*. New York: Teachers College Press.

Finders, M. 1997. *Just Girls: Hidden Literacies and Life in Junior High*. New York: Teachers College Press.

Freire, P. 1995. *Pedagogy of the Oppressed*. New York: Continuum.

Gardner, H. 1983. *Frames of Mind: The Theory of Multiple Intelligences*. New York: Basic.

———. 1993. *Multiple Intelligences: The Theory into Practice*. New York: Basic.

Gee, J. P. 1989 "Literacy, Discourse, and Linguistics: Introduction." *Journal of Education* 171: 5–25.

Gillespie, J. T. 2003. "A Brief Guide to Booktalking." In *Teenplots: A Booktalk Guide to Use with Readers Ages 12–18*, ed. J. T. Gillespie and C. J. Naden, xiii–xvi. Westport, CT: Libraries Unlimited.

Gillespie, J. T., and C. J. Naden. 2003. *Teenplots: A Booktalk Guide to Use with Readers Ages 12–18*. Westport, CT: Libraries Unlimited.

Hillocks, G. 1980. "Toward a Hierarchy of Skills in the Comprehension of Literature." *English Journal* 69: 54–59.

———. 1989. "Literary Texts in Classrooms." In *From Socrates to Software: The Teacher as Text and the Text as Teacher. 88th Yearbook of the National Society for the Study of Education*, ed. P. W. Jackson and S. Haroutunian-Gordon, 135–58. Chicago: University of Chicago Press.

———. 1995. *Teaching Writing as Reflective Practice*. New York: Teachers College Press.

Hunt, B., and T. Hunt. 2004. "Reading Successfully? Just What Does *Success* Mean, Anyway?" *English Journal* 98 (5): 95–99.

Hynd, C. 1999. "Instructional Considerations for Literacy in Middle and Secondary Schools: Toward an Integrated Model of Instruction." In *Engaged Reading: Processes, Practices, and Policy Implications*, ed. J. Guthrie and D. Alvermann, 81–104. New York: Teachers College Press.

Hynds, S. 1997. *On the Brink: Negotiating Literature and Life with Adolescents*. New York: Teachers College Press.

International Reading Association. 2000. *Excellent Reading Teachers: A Position Statement of the International Reading Association*. Retrieved May 5, 2005, from www.reading.org.

International Reading Association (IRA) and National Middle Schools Association (NMSA). 2002. *Supporting Young Adolescents' Literacy Learning*. Retrieved May 5, 2005, from www.reading.org/positions.html.

John-Steiner, V. 2000. *Creative Collaboration*. New York: Oxford University Press.

Kirby, D., and T. Liner. 1988. *Inside Out: Developmental Strategies for Teaching Writing*. Portsmouth, NH: Boynton/Cook.

Lamott, A. 1994. *Bird by Bird: Some Instructions on Writing and Life*. New York: Anchor.

Lesesne, T. S., and L. Buckman. 2001. "By Any Other Name: Reconnecting Readers in the High School." In *Teaching Reading in High School English Classes*, ed. Bonnie O. Ericson, 101–14. Urbana, IL: NCTE.

Marshall, J. D., P. Smagorinsky, and M. W. Smith. 1995. *The Language of Interpretation: Patterns of Discourse in Discussions of Literature*. Urbana, IL: NCTE.

McMahon, S. I., and T. E. Raphael. 1997. *The Book Club Connection: Literacy Learning and Classroom Talk*. New York: Teachers College Press.

McQuillan, J., with J. Beckett, L. Gutierrez, M. Rippon, S. Snyder, D. Wager, G. Williams, and E. Zajec. 2001. "If You Build It, They Will Come: A Book Flood for Struggling Readers in an Urban High School." In *Teaching Reading in High School English Classes*, ed. Bonnie O. Ericson, 69–83. Urbana, IL: NCTE.

Moore, D. W., T. W. Bean, D. Birdyshaw, and J. A. Rycik. 1999. *Adolescent Literacy: A Position Statement*. Newark, DE: International Reading Association.

Moore, E., and K. Stevens. 2004. *Good Books Lately: The One-Stop Resource for Book Groups and Other Greedy Readers*. New York: St. Martin's Griffin.

Moore, J. N. 1997. *Interpreting Young Adult Literature: Literary Theory in the Secondary Classroom*. Portsmouth, NH: Boynton/Cook.

National Council of Teachers of English (NCTE) and International Reading Association (IRA). 1996. *Standards for the English Language Arts*. Urbana, IL, and Newark, DE: NCTE and IRA.

National Council of Teachers of English (NCTE) Commission on Reading. 2004a. *A Call to Action: What We Know About Adolescent Literacy and Ways to Support Teachers in Meeting Students' Needs*. Retrieved May 5, 2005, from www.ncte.org/about/over/positions /category/read/118622.htm.

———. 2004b. *On Reading, Learning to Read, and Effective Reading Instruction: An Overview of What We Know and How We Know It*. Retrieved May 5, 2005, from www.ncte.org/about/over/positions /category/read/118620.htm.

National Council of Teachers of English Executive Committee. 1999. *NCTE Position Statement on Reading*. Retrieved May 5, 2005, from www.ncte.org/print.asp?id=107666@node=627.

Nystrand, M., with A. Gamoran, R. Kachur, and C. Prendergast. 1997. *Opening Dialogue: Understanding the Dynamics of Language and Learning in the English Classroom*. New York: Teachers College Press.

O'Donnell-Allen, C. 2005. "Pedagogical Recycling: How Colleagues Change Colleagues' Minds." *English Journal* 95 (2): 58–64.

O'Donnell-Allen, C., and P. Smagorinsky. 1999. "Revising Ophelia: Rethinking Questions of Gender and Power in School." *English Journal* 88: 35–42.

Oldfather, P. 1993. *Students' Perspectives on Motivating Experiences in Literacy Learning*. Perspectives in Reading Research No. 2. Athens, GA: Universities of Georgia and Maryland, National Reading Research Center.

Pennac, D. 1999. *Better than Life*. York, ME: Stenhouse.

Pratt, M. L. 1991. "Arts of the Contact Zone." In *Profession* 91: 33–40. New York: MLA.

Rabin, S. 1990. "Literature Study Groups: Teachers, Texts, and Readers." *English Journal* 79 (7): 41–46.

Richards, I. A. 1929. *Practical Criticism*. New York: Harcourt Brace Jovanovich.

Richison, J. D., A. C. Hernandez, and M. J. Carter. 2006. *Theme Sets for Secondary Students: How to Scaffold Core Literature*. Portsmouth, NH: Heinemann.

Richter, D. H. 2000. *Falling into Theory: Conflicting Views on Reading Literature*. 2nd ed. New York: Bedford/St. Martin's.

Robertson, S. L. 1998. "Using Dialectical Journals to Build Beginning Literary Response." In *Into Focus: Understanding and Creating Middle School Readers*, ed. K. Beers and B. G. Samuels, 199–222. Norwood, MA: Christopher-Gordon.

Romano, T. 1995. *Writing with Passion: Life Stories, Multiple Genres*. Portsmouth, NH: Heinemann.

Rosenblatt, L. 1938. *Literature as Exploration*. New York: D. Appleton-Century.

———. 1978. *The Reader, the Text, the Poem: The Transactional Theory of the Literary Work*. Carbondale, IL: Southern Illinois University Press.

Schoenbach, R., C. Greenleaf, C. Cziko, and L. Hurwitz. 1999. *Reading for Understanding: A Guide to Improving Reading in Middle and High School Classrooms*. San Francisco: Jossey-Bass.

Schön, D. 1987. *Educating the Reflective Practitioner: Toward a New Design for Teaching and Learning in the Professions*. San Francisco: Jossey-Bass.

Smagorinsky, P. 2002. *Teaching English Through Principled Practice*. Upper Saddle River, NJ: Merrill Prentice Hall.

Smagorinsky, P., T. McCann, and S. Kern. 1987. *Explorations: Introductory Activities for Literature and Composition, Grades 7–12*. Urbana, IL: NCTE.

Smagorinsky, P., and C. O'Donnell-Allen. 1998a. "The Depth and Dynamics of Context: Tracing the Sources and Channels of Engagement and Disengagement in Students' Response to Literature." *Journal of Literacy Research* 30: 515–59.

———. 1998b. "Reading as Mediated and Mediating Action: Composing Meaning for Literature Through Multimedia Interpretive Texts." *Reading Research Quarterly* 33: 198–226.

Smith, M. W., and J. Wilhelm. 2002. *"Reading Don't Fix No Chevys": Literacy in the Lives of Young Men*. Portsmouth, NH: Heinemann.

Soter, A. O. 1999. *Young Adult Literature and the New Literary Theories: Developing Critical Readers in Middle School*. New York: Teachers College Press.

Strickland, K., and J. Strickland. 1998. *Reflections on Assessment: Its Purposes, Methods and Effects on Learning*. Portsmouth, NH: Boynton/Cook.

True, J. 1979. "Round Robin Reading Is for the Birds." *Language Arts* 56: 918–21.

Underwood, W. 1987. "The Body Biography: A Framework for Student Writing." *English Journal* 76: 44–48.

Vygotsky, L. S. 1978. *Mind in Society: The Development of Higher Psychological Processes*. Cambridge, MA: Harvard University Press.

Wells, G. 1994. *Changing Schools from Within: Creating Communities of Inquiry.* Toronto: OISE.

———. 2001. *Action, Talk, and Text: Learning and Teaching Through Inquiry.* New York: Teachers College Press.

Wells, G., and G. L. Chang-Wells. 1992. *Constructing Knowledge Together: Classrooms as Centers of Inquiry and Literacy.* Portsmouth, NH: Heinemann.

Wilhelm, J. 1997. *"You Gotta BE the Book": Teaching Engaged and Reflecting Reading with Adolescents.* New York: Teachers College Press.

Wolf, D. P. 1988. *Reading Reconsidered: Literature and Literacy in High School.* New York: College Board.

# Index